2.95

W9-DJP-821

Americans Speak Out

Americans Speak Out

by
Charles E. Blair

MOODY PRESS

CHICAGO

Library of Congress Catalog Card Number: 79-181583

ISBN: 0-8024-0210-0

Printed in the United States of America

Contents

INTRODUCTION

While the orange-tinted eastern sky plays a silent yet moving prelude to a new day, a lone figure stands statue-still on a knoll overlooking the etched skyline of a sprawling metropolis, his head bowed in prayer. The praying man is Pastor Charles E. Blair; the spreading city is Denver, Colorado.

Charles Blair made an unprecedented move. He asked an independent research company to take an intensive random sampling of Denverites. The objective? To discover what Denver's man-on-the-street considers his foremost problems. Those receiving the most votes are the basis for this book.

Pastor Blair has served the Queen City of the Plains for a quarter of a century. With interdenominational Calvary Temple as a base, the fifty-one-year-old pastor and his 6,000 members use literally all of the modern media "to tell the old, old story of Jesus and His love."

Each weekday, Metro Denver enjoys Pastor Blair's "Counsel and Comment" radio talk program, when, by telephone, listeners can participate in the lively half-hour broadcast. Each Sunday, for an hour, the Rocky Mountain Empire views on color television one of Calvary Temple's three morning worship services.

Of every incoming dollar, 42 percent of it goes abroad to feed and clothe the world's destitute, as well as to fulfill Christ's command to saturate the earth with the Gospel. Calvary Temple supports eighty missionary families in sixty countries, in addition to financing church construction and various

1

other projects. 1980 goal: a CT representative in every free country of the world, with fifty cents of every dollar going to foreign missions.

Several CT nursing homes care for the aged of colorful Colorado. Life Center, designed eventually to accommodate 600 beds, is currently operating with 225 patients and a Christian staff that includes an M.D. and a psychologist. A psychiatrist and a chaplain will soon join the personnel. Life Center produces a television documentary series, "Better World," which features current events as they relate to Scripture.

Calvary Temple trains tomorrow's leaders in a well-organized and highly-departmentalized youth program. Almost every week, educational directors of churches from across the nation come to study CT's church school program. A full-time staff of twenty divisional directors and youth pastors—not to mention the army of lay leaders and teachers—sees to it that this "seminary" of 5,000 students operates efficiently and effectively.

This past year, while most churches were struggling through their annual "summer slump," CT attendance actually soared. Preaching or teaching, training or visiting, giving or praying, serving or caring, whatever it is—understandable or unexplainable —something wonderful, something special is happening at 200 South University Boulevard in Denver, Colorado.

1

"We've polluted everything from here to the moon."

Environmental pollution is as old as life itself. Moses was handling ecological problems when the children of Israel moved through the wilderness to the promised land. That was nearly 3500 years ago.

Today we are worried about the debris in outer space and on the moon. We put it there. We have a way of leaving a mess wherever we go. Waste and garbage disposal is big business.

We are now fighting for survival in defense against ourselves. Denverites believe environmental pollution is our most urgent problem. Of the respondents to the survey, 20 percent said that ecology was their main concern. No other sociological problem came anywhere near this percentage except family finances in second position with 16 percent. In an identical survey two and a half years ago (summer of 1968), pollution wasn't even mentioned.

"In the last few years environmental pollution has risen to a high place in the list of public concerns. This is the natural result of the worsening state of the environment—foul air in the cities, polluted streams and lakes in the countryside, unusable beaches on the shore, and everywhere mounting heaps of garbage and waste. People are increasingly aware of the harmful effects of environmental pollutants on their bodies. Smog and other air pollutants irritate the eyes and worsen respiratory diseases. Water pollution is a threat to health."[1]

We know that we are grappling with a problem of our own making, but we are not quite sure what it is, how to handle it, or that we really want to handle it at all.

There is no doubt in our minds that we are in serious trouble. We have unbalanced the ecosystem in nature. "Environmental pollution is grave evidence that our account books are badly out of balance—that wealth and prosperity have been gained at the cost of a huge, hidden, long-ignored debt to the environmental system that supports us. The rapidly mounting environmental crisis is a warning that we must now pay that debt, if we are to survive."[2]

Few of us realized and appreciated nature's built-in safeguards to survival and how we were capable of violating these delicate laws of nature. And now, almost too late, we see how nature and man are dependent upon each other.

"History shows the curious paradox of *man* as *part* of nature, and *man* as *apart* from nature—a force of geological magnitude, changing the face of the earth. Man has the power, now more than ever, to alter the landscape and to exterminate species of animals and plants that he does not like or does not find useful to his purposes. But, does he have the right? It has been suggested that one fault of ethical philosophy is that it has dealt *only* with relations of man to man, an almost totally man-centered value system. We need to develop a conscience beyond man—an 'ecological conscience.' "[3]

Activity on the ecological front in 1970 was widespread and impressive. In July, Charles Lindbergh expressed his feeling that governments should protect the environment to prevent the destruction of civilization. He called for worldwide environmental protection policy.

In July and August, United States and European Scientists held a month-long meeting (Aspen, Colorado) on global pollution and other environmental problems. Distinguished scientists, economists, historians and philosophers agreed that the human family is approaching a crisis, but there was disagreement on how to reach the desired goals.

A $5-million laboratory—Biotron—at Wisconsin University, is designed to simulate any environment on earth. The lab will help ecologists learn more about interaction between organisms and their physical surroundings.

In October, U Thant warned that U.N. members subordinate their ancient quarrels and launch an international effort to improve the environment within the next 10 years to avoid world catastrophe.

In November, the International Union of Conservation of Nature and the National Resources and Conservation Foundation officials began preparing an Ecological Guidebook for Development Planners to help developing nations avoid haphazard industrialization that has caused environmental problems in advanced nations.

Also in November, the Pope warned that rapid pollution of the environment may lead to ecological catastrophe. Apollo 11 astronaut N. A. Armstrong, first man to set foot on the moon, said the earth is an "oasis of life" that must be protected from environmental despoilation. Professor G. Wald (R.I.U.) warned that civilization will end within 15 to 30 years, unless immediate action is taken to solve pollution and other crucial world problems. He said that the quality of life has deteriorated during the 20th century.

In December, the U. S. Environmental Protection Agency conceded that the 1972 U.N. Conference on Human Environment will not find solutions to the major environmental problems, but it is hoped that international agreements will be ratified to control pollution and that international action and research programs will begin. Professor P. Ehrlich expressed his opinion that technology cannot save the world from ecological disaster, but felt that man can do it if he is willing to revise his economic thinking and alter his life style.

The State of Colorado is so concerned about ecological conditions that a commission (55 members) was appointed by the Governor and the General Assembly "to study the problems of the environment and to make recommendations concerning protection of the quality of that environment." Dangers were pointed out and sixteen recommendations were listed and explained. Two areas were of such an urgent nature that resolutions were passed.

Obviously, Denver doesn't want to become another New York City or a Los Angeles. "All America was once blessed with a desirable natural environment. Colorado's advantage is that its environment has not yet been destroyed by man. Three centuries ago Manhattan Island was a location extraordinarily blessed by beauty. Now it is at the nadir of the spiral of environmental deterioration. Only twenty years ago, Southern California represented the realization of the American dream, a realization based upon its environmental beauty. Today, Southern California, too, has descended the spiral to pollution, urban decay, and environmental destruction."[5]

Automobiles are blamed for a good percentage of the pollution in the Denver Metro Area. "Colorado also has a growing air pollution problem, especially in the major urban areas. Automobile exhaust is the major contribution to air pollution, including irritating and unesthetic photochemical smog. Thus, the more heavily we depend on the private car for transportation, the more cars there are on the road and the more polluted the air becomes. We must break out of this vicious circle of autos/highways/air pollution. Transportation in Colorado must be viewed as one integrated function."[6]

People who are pushing for pollution control believe the key is in the hand of the public. The pressure should come from the people. The legislation must not get bogged down by business interests or politics. "In their hurry to attain some ambition, to gratify the dream of a life, men often throw honor, truth and generosity to the winds. Politicians dare to stand by and see a city poisoned with foul water until they 'see where they come in' on a waterworks appropriation. If it be necessary to poison an army— that, too, is but an incident in the hurry for wealth."[7]

We are seeing some progress toward cleaner air and water. Engineers are exploring alternatives to the gasoline engine. Efforts are being concentrated on the battery and steam-powered cars. Factories are experimenting with filters both for waste and smoke.

A little less than half of us still smoke tobacco. This highly concentrated form of pollution and poisoning is still too popular. The habit dies slower than the people who serve it. King Nicotine still has many faithful subjects who will lay down their lives for him. During the past several years, many have realized that they owe nothing to the killer and have broken free. May their number increase with every clean breath.

The only "safe" and the only "clean" cigarette is the one that isn't smoked. "One cause of air pollution is carbon monoxide. This is a major pollutant from cigarette smoke. Actually, a smoker gets more carbon monoxide in his lungs when he smokes than is in the air of the most polluted city in the world on its worst day of pollution.

"I don't wish to deny the cigarette smoker's right to poor health, but it seems reasonable his rights should stop where the other person's rights begin."[8]

Francis A. Soper, Editor of the *Listen* Magazine, concludes his anti-smoking editorial: "In other words, your pollution should stop where my nose begins!"

A cigarette-smoking anti-pollution crusader reminds me of our inconsistency in other, more important areas. Mankind strives to eliminate physical disease, while he encourages every sort of ethical and moral pollution.

Jesus said it is not what goes into a man that defiles him, but what comes out of his heart. What good is a healthy body when the mind is polluted beyond hope?

We are so concerned about our physical spots and blemishes that we spend billions of dollars each year to cover them up. But what are we doing about soul pollution?

Man has been fairly successful in his efforts to control much of his environment: disease, natural disasters, population, production. *Self*-control is the area where no progress has been made. But the Bible clearly states that if we break moral laws, we will pay for it. We cannot get away with breaking natural laws, and this certainly holds true for spiritual laws.

While it is right to be concerned about the pollutants we take into our bodies, allow Jesus to remind us of the pollution that comes out of a man—out of his soul: "That which cometh out of the man, that defileth (pollutes) the man. For from within, out of the heart of men, proceed evil thoughts, adulteries, fornications, murders, thefts, covetousness, wickedness, deceit, lasciviousness, an evil eye, blasphemy, pride, foolishness; all these evil things come from within, and defile (pollute) the man" (Mark 7:20-23).

We are having ecological complications today because yesterday we did things without knowing the natural results of our actions. There is much that we do without considering the consequences. This never had to happen. If we had heeded the Bible's guidelines and warnings, we would have proceeded with wisdom and self-control, both in natural and in spiritual realms. Fortunately, it is still not too late.

[1]Barry Commoner, "Environmental Pollution," 1971 Edition *The World Almanac.* (Published by Newspaper Enterprise Association, Inc., New York), p. 462.
[2]Ibid, World Almanac, p. 464.
[3]"The Environment," *Colorado Environmental Commission,* Interim Report, December 1970, p. 5.
[4]Op. cit., *Colorado Environmental Commission,* p. 1.
[5]Ibid. p. 7.
[6]Ibid, p. 12.
[7]William G. Jordan, *Self-Control: Its Kingship and Majesty,* (Fleming H. Revell Co., New York, 1905), pp. 117-118.
[8]Editorial, *Listen,* January, 1971.

2

"How can I make ends meet?"

"My number one problem? . . . Just making ends meet!"

Are these the words of the unemployed?—the disadvantaged?—the residents of a poverty-stricken area?

Not necessarily. These words echo the concern of people living in Denver, Colorado, a city where per capita income ranks among the highest in the nation, a segment of society which is apparently prosperous and affluent, yet plagued by financial worries! Of those responding to the survey, 16 percent said inflation/finances is their number one problem.

With a mere 6 percent of the population of the world, the United States has fifteen times more goods than all the rest of the world put together. But in spite of the highest standard of living of any nation on earth, many families in this country are burdened with debts and are without savings of any kind.

The difficulties become most obvious around the first of the month when a stack of bills is compared to the balance in the checkbook. The early months of the year are often especially difficult with the additional expenses of taxes, automobile licenses, insurance premiums, and the reminders of the extravagance of Christmas shopping the previous year.

Why is this so? What can be done about it? The solution to any problem can only be found by analyzing its cause and deciding where to go from there. So we must ask ourselves: Where does the money go? How can we best manage our affairs? Why do we have these problems? What are God's suggestions?

Where Does Money Go?

Most people do not know where their dollars go. Since they get rid of it "a little here and a little there," before they know, it's gone! Although they might know what was paid for the family car, the television set, and a few major items, most people have no real idea of what happens to their money.

Four Major Expenses

According to the Statistical Bureau in Washington, D. C., we spend more on the *maintenance of our homes* than on any other single item. Rent, interest, mortgage payment, utilities, repairs, furnishings, equipment that is needed for the operation of the home, and taxes rank first in expenditures. The larger the income, the more expensive the things that are purchased. One man said, "The higher the standard of living, the more ways there are of becoming poor." At every level of income, the fact remains that home expenditures occupy first place.

The second highest expense to the income is the *cost of food*. Each family should ascertain its own individual expenditures to include groceries, entertainment of guests, and the inevitable treat—eating out. Most problems incurred in this area could be solved with the "waste not—want not" method. Charles H. Spurgeon is quoted as saying, "Hundreds would never have known want if they had not at first known waste."[1] The Prodigal Son " 'wasted his substance with riotous living.' He spent not only his money—but his substance. . . . There is always a 'mighty famine' just around the corner of Spendthrift Boulevard. It is a short journey from the residence of 'Riotous Living' to the shack of 'Poverty'."[2]

The third highest expense is *transportation*. Now, don't get taken for a ride here! Since approximately eighty out of every one hundred Americans have at least one car, it is likely that the purchase of an automobile will become your concern also. Before you buy, get the facts so you won't come down with new car fever. "The best time to buy is when you shop armed with information about the car you need, how much you can afford (including financing, insurance and maintenance costs) . . ."[3] Remember: "Just because a man passes you with his car is no sign that he isn't behind with his payments."[4] Therefore, let caution, instead of pride, attend the purchase of your transportation requirements.

Ranking fourth in importance is the *cost of clothing*. Approximately $10 out of every $100 is spent "to be fashionably covered." Unfortunately, what we need has little to do with what we want. And we are often tempted to let our wants determine our spending. No two people need the same amount of clothing, so it is necessary that each home fit its individual requirements.

The Credit Trap

A University of Michigan survey has stated that one-half of the nation's families has some kind of an installment payment or debt. A pocketful of credit cards is "a way to buy miracles on time—or misery in installments. Charging and more charging can leave you forever paying for clothes that don't fit any more, Christmas toys that were bought last year, and meals you don't even remember. How much credit, then, can you afford? The answer is only what you can pay when due out of your income . . ."[5]

We ". . . must face the fact that credit buying is here to stay. It is an accepted part of our successful economy. Paying for credit—that is, paying interest charges—is no less honorable today than paying for food, clothing, and shelter."[6] But here is the danger: Approximately one out of every ten families is committed to an indebtedness of 20 percent of their income. They owe one-fifth of their earnings before they even receive their pay check.

A survey in 1968 determined that almost 80 percent of the average family's income was spent in the four categories: shelter, food, transportation, and clothing. Add to this the money spent for credit purchases of previous months. Then include the expenses of medical care, education, recreation, and giving to benevolent and church organizations, and one can understand how our total amount of money "goes up in smoke." Furthermore, it becomes obvious that there is frequently nothing to save for future emergencies. "If your outgo exceeds your income, then your upkeep will be your downfall."

The Cares of Life

In Luke 8:14, Jesus speaks of the word of God being *choked with cares and riches and pleasures of this life*. Here the original word for life is "bios" and it refers to the necessities of everyday life. "The cares of life" would include the worry about paying monthly bills. These include the house payment,

13

food, utilities, and clothes. They also include payments on new items, appliances, insurance, toys, vacations, recreation, medical and dental expenses, and other items—all a part of daily life.

It is acceptable to want to have enough money to carry out specific, worthy goals. To provide one's family with a comfortable and happy life is a reasonable goal. But one must draw the line between what one needs and what one wants. Because of his concern for life's necessities and worldly things, a man's heart could be drawn from the spiritual way of life to a preoccupation with money. "For the love of money is the first step toward all kinds of sin. Some people have even turned away from God because of their love for it, and as a result have pierced themselves with many sorrows" (1 Timothy 6:10, LNT).

How Can We Best Manage Our Affairs?

Management means the manner of handling, regulating, administrating, and superintending. It means planning. And planning means budgeting. It is wise to decide where we need to spend our money to accomplish our purposes as a family and then set up a *budget* for the future.

Who Is the Boss?

A serious question to be answered is who should manage the affairs of the house. Leadership is always acknowledged in successful homes. But who is going to supervise? And in what areas? We generally get the concept that there is one head in each house. Not necessarily so. Just as in business, I believe there can be a working relationship in home management.

Often the father has the main job outside the

home, while the mother has the chief job inside. However, increasingly today, many women work outside the home and are responsible for part of the income required in the operation of their homes. In either case, there is a cooperative job for each. The home can be run under joint management.

Team Work

If differences develop in some areas, it is essential to keep the lines of communication open. Marriage is "for better or for worse," so a divorce just because of financial problems is not part of the agreement. Keep objectives out in the open and maintain clear and prompt communication. If adjustments need to be made, make them objectively and in the spirit of teamwork. Don't try to keep secrets but discuss everything pertaining to home finances above the table.

Why Do We Have These Problems?

I believe I can sum up the answer to that question in three ways: indecision about purpose, unwise competition with others, and failure to accept individual responsibility. Solving these errors will go far in restoring a harmonious financial relationship in marriage.

Goals Out of Focus

First of all, if you are going to manage anything, you have to come to grips with what you believe. In other words, ask the question, "What is the purpose of this home?" Agree on a philosophy based on your mutual ambitions and abilities. What size family are you going to have? What are your financial horizons? Decide not only how the physical home is to be built,

15

and how financing will be managed, but also on the pervading atmosphere.

Living Within Means

Most people endeavor to "keep up with the Joneses." Some, of course, try to keep up with just about everybody! Speaking not only from the experience within my own home, but from the experience I've gained in counseling many lives that crossed my pathway as a pastor, I urge you not to do something simply because somebody else does it. There is no point to spending more than you make on things you don't need in order to impress people you don't like!

Young people, be careful that you don't feel that you've come down in the world when you purchase less expensive items than your Mom and Dad own. To live within your means is to follow the Christian philosophy, "Not that I was ever in need, for I have learned how to get along happily whether I have much or little" (Philippians 4:11, LNT).

Rejecting Responsibility

The third problem in the management of family finance is that every member may not be shouldering his share of responsibility. In order to keep the established objectives for your home and to live within the family budget, every member must do all that he or she is expected to do to make the plan work. With God as the "Senior Partner" and the clear objective to do His will, there is little excuse for anyone, parent or child, not to do his own part. I suggest that each motive, each responsibility, each relationship be examined; then, work toward those goals—together, not sloughing off individual responsibilities.

Quibbling

Management and human relations always go together. Some people reduce the home environment to that portrayed several years ago by a radio family called the Bickersons. Bickering was the theme of that household, and little things always started the breakdown of their relationship. I recommend that every home set its ground rules and then keep them. The responsibility to follow these rules should be considered a privilege.

What Are God's Suggestions?

Stewardship (superintending that which God has given us) begins with the Christian conviction that all of life is a trust. Everything we have, and everything we shall have, is the result of God's generosity toward us. Since everything that is "ours" was originally His, we are accountable to God.

A Productive Life

As good stewards of that which God entrusts to our care, we must determine to buy up every opportunity to make life productive. A productive life will bring honor and glory to God, and in turn the good steward will be blessed for his faithfulness. Man does not want just to vegetate; he wants to live, to work, to love, and to feel that life is worthwhile. Proper appropriation of our money is the measure of our stewardship. And I believe the reason that God deals with this touchy subject—money—is because He knows it is the index of our character!

"Jesus was deeply concerned about the way people made and used their money. Throughout the Four Gospels one verse in every eight deals with the proper use of material possessions, and sixteen out of the thirty-eight parables deal with the same theme. His main concern was that in making money people should not lose their manhood. He warned them that it can be secured at too high a price and that one makes a bad bargain if he gets money in such a way that he loses his soul or harms the soul of his neighbor."[7]

To me the "foundation plank" on which a happy home can stand is a well-planned system of priorities. In deciding on family goals, we must decide what comes first. A selfish goal in first place will never bring a happy home.

Our financial planning is a good indicator of our priorities. The check stub is a good index to our own way of life. If you gave me your check stubs which cover the last twelve months, I could write a true story of your interests. We spend our money where our concerns are. We become, as someone has well said, what we care about most. If I am a golfer, then I invest in golfing equipment. If I am a fisherman, I buy fishing equipment.

Who Is Really First?

If 6 percent of our income is spent on cigarettes and 1 percent is left for God, we must recognize that we love ourselves more. On the other hand, if the *first* ten cents out of every dollar are given to God, the ninety cents will go further than the one hundred cents spent on self. I cannot explain it, but I can tell you that IT WORKS! It is no guarantee for becoming wealthy, and God's formula of the tithe was never intended for that. God may even test us financially *while* we tithe. Ultimately, I believe, the road will turn and all will come back—houses and lands —as we give.

Remember Tomorrow

I have a second suggestion for families that wish to go God's financial way. After you've given God the first ten cents, put another dime away for a rainy day. Then live on the budgeted remaining eighty cents from every dollar. Begin to plan for that which will someday mean more to you than just what you now see. Our values change as we grow older. I'm deeply grateful to the one who taught that principle to me. A rainy day just might be that unexpected emergency that usually happens to the other family.

The great missionary to Africa, David Livingstone, stated: "I will place no value on anything that I have or possess except in relation to the Kingdom of Christ. If anything I have will advance that Kingdom, it shall best be given or kept, as by giving or keeping it I shall best promote the glory of Him to whom I owe all my hopes for both time and eternity."

[1]George M. Bowman, "Waste Not—Want Not," *Here's How to Succeed with Your Money* (Chicago: Moody Press, 1960), p. 91.
[2]Ibid., p. 93.
[3]*Everybody's Money,* (Madison, Wisconsin: CUNA International, Inc. 1970).
[4]*Changing Times.*
[5]Op. cit., *Everybody's Money,* pp. 22-23.
[6]George M. Bowman, "Buying ·on Credit," *Here's How to Succeed with Your Money* (Chicago: Moody Press, 1960), p. 46.
[7]Walter Dudley Cavert, "The Christian and His Money," *Remember Now . . .* (New York: Abingdon Press, 1944), p. 141.

3

"I don't expect peace from people."

Will the time ever come when men will "learn war no more?" Will war ever become extinct?

People have been killing each other ever since Cain killed Abel. No one seems to want war, but everybody is doing it—on a lesser or greater scale. Whether it is psychological warfare between political ideologies, armed conflict between aggressive nations, or dissension in the family, we just can't seem to have peace on earth. Why?

During the last nine years (from January 1, 1961 through November 7, 1970), 43,959 American servicemen have died in Vietnam. In 1968, the Southeast Asian conflict was the main concern of 25 percent of the people polled. In other words, the quest for peace was the Number One Problem at that time. In January, 1971, this category slipped down to the number three position, with only 12 percent of the respondents showing a primary interest in Vietnam.

It seems that war is always with us and peace is an illusive dream. But mankind has never given up hope for lasting peace. The twentieth century was supposed to have been the Christian Century but was ushered in by the Boer War. The future seemed bright—until 1914. The League of Nations was established in 1920, and it was proclaimed that World War I was the war that was going to end all other wars. World War II shattered this claim, and the

20

League of Nations was finally disbanded in 1946.

I was in San Francisco when President Harry S. Truman arrived for the signing of the preamble to the United Nations Charter. Surely, this new and powerful organization would, once and for all, outlaw aggression and war! That was more than 25 years ago. We have had nothing but continuous conflict: India-China, India-Pakistan, China-Tibet, Russia-China, Arab-Israel, Congo-Biafra and endless unrest and revolution in both hemispheres.

The Institute for Statistics Studies (London) calls this the "Age of Conflict." This non-Christian group has discovered that wars are actually more frequent. Seventy-three of 120 conflicts have occurred *since* the close of World War II.

In spite of this, mankind works and hopes for peace. Some think, because we are making progress in science and technology, that before long we will find the secret to real peace.

Is It Always Sinful to Wage War?

It was Benjamin Franklin who said, "There never was a good war or a bad peace." But while the police officer takes no pleasure in enforcing the peace, the work of law enforcement must be done, or evil will triumph over good. So in war. Americans are a peace-loving people, but we will refuse even peace on the terms of those who want to bring peace by imprisoning the human race under a diabolical ideology. We want peace but not without freedom.

"Christianity is alien to pessimism about man and to irrationalism about history. Rather, it declares that the Christian is a citizen of two worlds. He owes his first allegiance to Christ and His Kingdom; but he

21

owes allegiance also to the community which secures for him his rights and privileges. To the Corinthians, Paul uttered a sharp rebuke when they interpreted his teaching as meaning that they should abstract themselves from the world altogether. For the Christian there will always be this fundamental tension between two loyalties, though the tension will express itself in different ways according to the changing patterns of social structure . . ."[1]

Said C. C. Colton: "War kills men, and men deplore the loss; but war also crushes bad principles and tyrants, and so saves societies." Augustine said: "True religion does not look upon as sinful those wars that are waged, not for motives of cruelty, but with the object of securing peace, or of punishing evildoers and of uplifting and doing good."

No, war is never desirable, but as long as men have war in their hearts, as long as men's hearts are wicked, there will be war. "There is no peace, saith the Lord, unto the wicked" (Isaiah 48:22).

Waging war is not always wrong. It would be as sinful to allow the spread of evil aggression as it would be to allow a polio epidemic to spread.

Does God Have Anything to Do with War?

I have stood on the front lines of Vietnam's battlefields. I have viewed the ugly material destruction. I have seen the scarred bodies stacked like cordwood. I was reminded that the heart is a rebel, that war is a result of sin. "War is a curse of mankind because he will not listen to God's will. War is the agony of mankind because he will not love his neighbor."[2]

Is God a warmonger, is He helpless to intervene or is He disinterested in the affairs of men? The Bible clearly teaches that God is in full control at all times. Nothing happens without His permission, and everything is happening according to His long-range plan. We need to keep in mind that God's ways and thoughts are completely different from ours.

The fallen Lucifer is still ". . . the prince of this world . . ." but even he is under God's constant control, while he tries to control the fallen angels that followed him. ". . . behind every earthly power there is a satanic power lurking, seeking to control and dominate for the glory of the rebel who declared war against God. We are not to be misled by the assertion that 'the powers that be are ordained of God' (Romans 13:1). All that Satan has done or is doing or will do is by the permissive will of God, who, since the Lord Jehovah is both omniscient and omnipotent, was certainly never astonished by the outbreak of Satan. It will become increasingly clear that Satan is working within the limits of the eternal plan of God."[3]

Who Is Our Real Enemy?

Basically, we are in spiritual warfare. There can be no lasting peace until all rebellion against God is removed. Every effort for world peace must be exhausted by both Satan and man before God will terminate the rebellion. Only then will the Prince of Peace establish His eternal kingdom. Augustine's now-famous prayer says, "Oh, God, Thou hast formed us for Thyself; and our souls can know no rest until they rest in Thee."

That God cares for us was proven at Calvary. But God is not limited by short-sightedness. He knows the end from the beginning. He is aware of all the

23

ramifications of every situation and every action. "God, man or the devil: these are the three possible sources of hope. The strategy of the invisible warfare has been planned by God in order that these questions shall be answered, once and for all, in the presence of all created beings whether human, celestial or infernal. Human history is the record of the attempts of man and Satan to do something for man. When asked why an omnipotent God permits the holocaust of human history, the answer from the Word of God must be that He permits it in order to demonstrate to the universe that neither Satan nor man can do anything for themselves or for each other."[4]

Not all men are under the control of Satan's will. Even the evil spiritual forces seem to be divided. The way of pride and willfulness can never succeed. No matter how hard Satan tries to unite the nations, recent history, especially the surprising events of World War II, proves his impotence. Men are not interested in God's will, but neither are very many interested in Satan's will. ". . . we have turned every one to his own way . . ." (Isaiah 53:6). As long as man is motivated by pride, peace is an impossibility.

For many millenniums Satan has been trying vainly to organize his crumbling kingdom. Futilely, his subordinates have been endeavoring to form a one-world government. The ninth chapter of Daniel reveals significant information about Satan's power structure in the atmosphere. We learn that evil "princes" are assigned to each earthly nation for the purpose of materializing Satan's objectives for this part of God's universe. We can count on this sort of an arrangement until the inauguration of the Kingdom of Peace.

"And I saw three unclean spirits like frogs come out of the mouth of the dragon, and out of the mouth of the beast, and out of the mouth of the false prophet. For they are the spirits of devils, working miracles, which go forth unto the kings of the earth and of the whole world, to gather them to the battle of that great day of God Almighty" (Rev. 16:13,14).

Even secular minds are considering the possibility of the existence and influence of extraordinary, invisible beings. We can no longer ridicule the belief in a spirit world. Much that has happened can be explained in no other way, not only in the actions of individuals but also in the unbelievable change of attitudes of entire nations.

Charles McIlwain, in an excellent book entitled *Constitutionalism and the Changing World,* made this profound statement: "When a great cultural nation like modern Germany suddenly turns its back on the principles held foremost for hundreds of years, there must be a cause, and it must be a cause lying deeper than the mere mentality of German leaders."[5] Mr. McIlwain is saying that there must be a force at work that is deeper and stronger than the minds of the German leaders, to cause that nation to follow Hitler after following Christ for centuries under the leadership of Martin Luther.

Why Do We Go to War?

We are fighting for something more precious than peace. As a nation, we are fighting Satanic forces "without and within." While we endeavor to frustrate the influence of "the Evil One" abroad, we are battling him on many fronts in the homeland. The celestial rebel is fighting God in the homes, in the schools, in the courts and in the government. The master deceiver simply wants to discredit God's goodness whenever and wherever possible.

Will There Ever Be Peace on Earth?

Yes! But only when the Prince of Peace returns. "Of the increase of his government and peace there shall be no end, upon the throne of David, and upon his kingdom, to order it, and to establish it with judgment and with justice from henceforth even for ever. The zeal of the Lord of hosts will perform this" (Isaiah 9:7).

Jesus made it clear that we would ". . . hear of wars and rumors of wars . . ." until His second coming. To the very end "nation shall rise against nation, and kingdom against kingdom" (Matthew 24:6,7). Man's efforts toward "one world" will never materialize. In the meantime we can have "peace with God" and the "peace of God" which surpasses human comprehension. And let us not forget to continue to pray, "Thy kingdom come; thy will be done on earth as it is in heaven."

[1]William Robinson, *The Devil and God*, (Abingdon-Cokesbury Press, New York, MCMXLV), p. 107.
[2]Air Force Major Victor Colasuonno (killed in action in Vietnam) "Voice from Grace," *The Denver Post*, Feb. 20, 1969, p. 13.
[3]Donald Grey Barnhouse, *The Invisible War*, (Zondervan Publishing House, Grand Rapids, Michigan, 1965), p. 23.
[4]Ibid, p. 94.
[5]Charles Howard McIlwain, *Constitutionalism and the Changing World*, (Cambridge University Press, 1969).

4

"The kids have found that affluence isn't the answer."[1]

"They (teenagers) are the most competent generation we have ever reared in this country—and the most maligned."—Harvard Professor Jerome Bruner.

Too many of us, I believe, have characterized as "unfortunate" the words and actions of the now generation. I say it is fortunate. It is fortunate that they are questioning just about everything. We taught them to think, and now we wish they wouldn't think so much. They may not be experts (they do not claim to be), but they are questioning the effectiveness of our social institutions.

If we are right, we have nothing to fear. But if we are wrong, we should be grateful to those who point out the error of our ways. Still, only 10 percent of those surveyed considered youth problems number one on their horizon.

Most fortunate is the fact that they are not only questioning the validity of our beliefs and practices, but they are also asking important questions about themselves. This makes me optimistic about the future.

In sizing up today's average young person, this is what I see: He is an idealist and cannot stand contradictions. Prejudice is scorned by him. Hypocrisy enrages him. He cannot tolerate complacency in the face of need.

If our society fosters injustices, we can count on our idealistic youth to reveal and condemn those injustices. The now generation doesn't claim to have all the answers. But it does see social inequity, and it does expect rectification—now. These young people are not impressed with the resolutions we passed at the last convention; they want on-the-spot solutions.

In the light of all this, it may be well for us to ask ourselves: Did we help to put the gap between our youth and ourselves? Are we forcing our young people to rebel?

I believe there are three areas in which adult America has failed its youth: (1) Example; (2) Enlightenment; (3) Conversion.

Youth Insists on Good Example

"They have the outrageous temerity to insist that individuals and societies live by the values they preach."—Kenneth Keniston[2]

Daily, we all either speak, read or write about the problems of youth. Adults blame the younger generation, decorating it generously with descriptive name labels. Youth throws the blame back to the adult, throwing in four-letter words for good measure. On which side is truth and who is on truth's side?

What are the adult concerns in relationship to the alienated generation? Some adults are saying that our young people are getting in with the wrong crowd, that they show lack of respect for their elders and for the law, are rebellious, have loose morals and lack discipline.

When speaking of adults, the young people point to hypocrisy, a double-standard, social injustices, complacency, lack of communication and love.

While both are right, the greater responsibility rightfully falls on the adult—on the parent, on the educator, on the public servant and community leader. Why should we expect our offspring to respect us and our laws if we are breaking the laws ourselves? Why should we expect our children to respect us while they watch us lie, cheat and steal? How can our youth respect government officials who daily deal in graft and corruption? Doesn't respect have to be earned? What kind of delinquency are we concerned about—that of the youth or that of the adult?

Mortimer Feinberg says: "The kids, with their heightened appreciation of the self, with their empathy and their idealism, have shaken us up and made some of us at least take a new look at our own shortcomings. If we were to act like the grownups we believe ourselves to be, it is quite possible that the example we set will be attractive enough to emulate. Kids have, in their favor, a tendency to be responsive to responsibility."[3]

Evangelist Billy Graham, knowing youth as he does, speaks in the same vein: "There is no doubt about it, we have given wrong values to our young people. We have taken the line that man can live by materialism alone, and now we're suddenly finding out that he cannot."[4]

Writing in *Christianity Today,* Robert J. Bartel refers to a survey taken by *Fortune Magazine.* He says: "An important conclusion of the *Fortune* study was that there is substantial rejection of traditional American values by the 'forerunner' group. Over two-thirds of the students surveyed in both categories ('practical-minded' and 'forerunners') would welcome less emphasis on status.

"If students have rejected much of the mainstream of traditional American values, what is the alternative they seek?

"They are concerned about the quality and condition of human existence and are willing to work for improvement. They want responsibility and not necessarily power."⁵

Asks Sam Levenson in *Everything But Money:* "Instead of challenging them with great causes, have we encouraged them to tinker with trifles?"

At no time do I justify the wrong attitudes and actions of youth, and least of all college students. "Two wrongs don't make a right," even if the first wrong was done by an adult. I am trying to bring in—as evidence—the things that confuse and frustrate our children and young people. They know what alcohol can do in the home and on the highway. They are aware of the crippling and killing power of tobacco. And they find it extremely difficult to follow the logic of a drinking, smoking parent who tells them not to smoke marijuana. A pill-popping parent (even if it's only a tranquilizer) can't be very convincing to his child who is on "speed."

We are never going to straighten out our youth until we bring ourselves in line. Too many of our social problems and evils are a direct result of our own "cheating on the test"—morally and spiritually. We cannot blame our children for refusing to build their future on the flimsy foundation we are providing them.

It should be clear that many of the undesirable youth trends can be re-routed by a good example on the part of adults. We can lead them only by proper example. We must go before them and show the way.

Youth Demands Enlightenment

In the words of the rich young ruler, the now generation is asking: "What lack I yet?" (Matthew 19:20). During the Christmas holidays we had several of our own C. T. college students participate in a discussion on our daily Counsel and Comment radio program. Here are some of the comments made by these perceptive young people:

"The average college student today does not know life's meaning or purpose. Professors, while they do impart knowledge, do not give real answers to the questions that concern students most."

Another of our young people said: "The general outlook among students is one of confusion and despair. The typical college student is lonely and searching for involvement in and commitment to something worthwhile. Unfortunately, most campus groups have a negative philosophy. They analyze institutions, find fault with them and are ready to destroy them, without being prepared to replace them with something better. None of these groups have a big following because the seeking student is soon disillusioned by the inconsistency and hypocrisy of the leaders."

It is in this environment that our youth turn to experimentation in the occult and with drugs. They search for truth everywhere. If they fail to understand themselves or the world, if they fail in their effort to improve it, and if they do not commit suicide, they will try any escape, including drugs, sex and leftist movements "Fun" may become their main goal.

Billy Graham observes: "Young people today are on a mad quest for purpose, for meaning, for fulfillment."[6]

E. Beatrice Batson, Professor at Wheaton College, compares the contemporary student with a John Bunyan searching for truth.[7] "Two of the most pressing questions for the contemporary student—indeed for all mankind—are, 'What situation am I in?' and 'Where do I go from here?' "[8]

Understanding stops where communication breaks down. Some years ago, the New York City Youth Board promoted a poster with this text: "When Family Life Stops, Delinquency Starts." I believe crime begins in the area of omission—when we fail to enlighten, to inform our children and our youth. Ignorance paves the way for much of the juvenile delinquency. Ignorance is weakness; enlightenment is power. Keeping kids in ignorance is criminal. Children are ours to inform. Information can avert the need for reformation. Information enlightens the mind. This in turn produces confidence. Confidence develops identity. The search for identity—self-actualization, self-esteem, belongingness—is crucial.

Why do some parents wait to discuss certain things until *after* their children have gotten into trouble? Why not "rap" with kids about our current VD epidemic? Why not communicate to them our fear of an epidemic of pot dropouts in the 1970's because of cannabism? "Cannabism (marijuana is a derivative of the cannabis plant) leads to the dropout syndrome, ending in a skid-row existence," doctors say.[9] If I were a foreign enemy power, I could not think of a more clever plan to incapacitate the "red-blooded" youth of our land than by the degenerating effects of drugs.

When Dr. Benjamin Spock says in the newspapers "It may be a wholesome thing"[10] for college students who are mature enough, to live together without being married, why not discuss this with teenagers while you as a parent can still make a contribution to the discussion? Putting good books into the hands of our children is commendable, but this does not take the place of person-to-person discussion.

Another area that needs discussion in the Christian home is the anti-Bible "hostility that permeates the entire academic community," as reported by college senior, Bill Meldon. "I recently glanced through several college library magazines. In each, I found some derogatory reference to Christ and Christianity."[11] Is your teenager mentally, emotionally and spiritually prepared for what awaits him on the college campus and in the classroom?

The now generation expects explicitness of belief, forthrightness in communication, and non-condescension in attitude.

Several years ago, *The New York Mirror*[12] listed ten positive steps which can be taken to nip delinquency at home before it flowers. The recommendations were made by boys who had gotten into trouble. Notice that the ten steps are timeless:

1. Don't be too easy with us. Don't give us our own way too much. Don't give us everything we want, when we want it.

2. Maintain firm discipline at home, but keep it fair. Don't keep changing the rules.

3. Keeping the family together is more important than keeping up with the Joneses. Let us know we can come to Mom and Pop with our problems. Make us feel wanted.

33

4. Show us how to make a living, how to get along with others in school and in business.
5. Don't let us get away with breaking the law or breaking family rules of discipline. Be strict. Give us privileges, but first make us earn them.
6. See our side too in arguments. Sit down and reason with us.
7. Watch the crowd we run around with. Let us bring our friends home. Meet them. Get to know them.
8. Don't let us stay out at all hours of the night. Set a time when we have to be home and make us stick to it.
9. Don't spare the rod. When we rate a wallop, don't hold back.
10. Cut down on activities that don't include the family. Give us more attention. Spend more time at home—with us.

Significant is the fact, as pointed out by Kenneth Keniston, a psychologist at Yale Medical School, that: "Most unalienated young people want large families; they marry early and are prepared to work hard to make their marriage a success; they usually value family life far more than meaningful work. Families play a special role in American life today—and among the reasons for our increasing emphasis on them is that they provide a place where a man can be himself and enjoy himself *in the present*. A wife and children can be enjoyed in the here and now, and are dependent neither on traditional wisdom nor on future success. Furthermore, children constitute a link with the future that, unlike vocational commitment, will endure regardless of change."[13]

Said educator Clark Kerr: "Spend time, not money." Affluence has not helped the family unit, it has weakened it. It is well for us to ask: Does my child feel and know that he is an important part of the family?

Let's not stop doing meaningful things together— games, hikes, building projects, political debates. Prolonged dinners bring out tensions. Too many parents are preoccupied with other things, with no time for their most priceless possession—their children. Some fathers hardly see their kids all week. The average family dinner lasts ten to twenty minutes even when the family does eat together.

Youth Requires Moral Reconstruction

Our survey showed that what young people want more than anything else is to learn from the pulpit "how to live." The survey also confirmed the fact that young people want rules and standards. Firm authority is a necessity of no lesser importance than love. Although children test our rules, they do expect to find something there to test, and they are depending on the guidelines not to give under pressure. The pushing is a natural part of developing distinct identity. But all too often, when they look for the rules, they just aren't to be found. This can be a traumatic experience.

Exactly what happens when parents abandon the Bible as a guide to living? Confusion abounds. All this is the result of the absence of a moral and spiritual foundation. The youth turn to the occult and to oriental religions to find truth. Even Jesus is being re-examined. "New songs about Jesus are filling the air. Rock. Hard rock, collectively, 'Jesus Rock' is being interpreted as reflection of a non-traditional religious quest among young people."[14]

Commenting on Decca's album, "Jesus Christ, Superstar," a reviewer in *Christianity Today* said: "Is Christ the Son of God or is he merely a prophet-man, no greater than Buddha or Mohammed? This generation longs for the answers."[15]

In the meantime, everybody wants to do their own thing. Tom Skinner, black evangelist in Harlem, points out the fallacy of "doing your thing," because of man's inevitable tendency to do the wrong thing. This is confirmed by Apostle Paul in Romans 7:18: "For I know that in me . . . dwelleth no good thing."

In a sane and searching article,[16] John W. Alexander, president of Inter-Varsity Christian Fellowship, points out that campus unrest has root reasons far deeper than are usually admitted in print today. In discussing the situation he says: "The cure is not a laundry job on dirty clothes, a paint job on rotting wood. We must change the central nature of individual man—change from a self-centered person incapable of much genuine love and riddled with greed and hate. The Bible speaks of this issue—clearly, simply, precisely. It presents the only long-term effective cure: The placing of a new nature inside man as individuals. God imparts the nature of Jesus Christ to individual men and women who choose to receive Him."

The following fact has never been disproved. When Jesus Christ is put to a valid test in an individual's life, in every case without exception, He gives the person true identity, full satisfaction and unreserved acceptance. In addition to this, the individual receives only the best motivation for living and only the most worthy purpose for existence.

Christ's superior power can break the power of any human habit. Those who have put Him to a fair and honest test, have discovered that His presence in their lives can replace all the harmful tranquilizers and energizers, all the dangerous barbiturates and amphetamines. We are told to "be strong in the Lord, and in the power of his might" (Ephesians 6:10). "He giveth his beloved sleep" (Psalm 127:2). Or, He can keep us awake and even give "in the night his song" (Psalm 42:8). All this should not surprise us, since "the body is . . . for the Lord; and the Lord for the body" (1 Corinthians 6:13).

Christ does not go after the surface symptoms. He does not stop with driving drugs and pornography out of a community. He gives the individual a new nature and makes him a new person, so that he is no longer in the market for such things.

Denominational differences aside, Jesus Christ's life and teaching alone are worthy of anyone's loyalty and devotion.

An honest, non-hypocritical Christian *can* attract others to God's good life. A vibrant, genuine Christian can go after the militants, the rebels, the revolutionaries and the dropouts by drawing attention to Christ's consistency and by introducing these desperate seekers to Him personally. We can challenge them to put the Risen Lord to the test. What have they got to lose? Christ is big enough for anybody and his needs. God gives His word of honor that in Christ we become *complete*. (See Colossians 2:10; 4:12). Christ is Creator and He is the strongest force that can be activated in a human life. The powerful presence of the Spirit of Christ is only good—it regenerates, it renews, it restores, it reconstructs, it rehabilitates. "All things are become new" (2 Corinthians 5:17).

Since the bad news grabs most of the headlines, we can be misled to believe that a high percentage of the nation's young people are in some sort of trouble or are generally rebelling against the establishment *per se*. But, upon reflecting, we know that this cannot be true. "According to the Educational Testing Service, only two percent of the students in colleges and universities belong to groups of the radical left."[2]

We know of the dedicated young people in our high schools and colleges. We see and hear them speak up and sing out for Christ and country, though you'll seldom read it in your daily paper.

There is real hope for America because we have so many genuine young people who cannot help but change the suicidal trends of some segments of today's America.

As I take a perspective view of America's future, I feel optimistic. I believe that God Himself has been using our youth to force adult America to take a realistic look at her moral and material self. And God may very well use our youth to bring about the nationwide spiritual rehabilitation that we so desperately need.

[1]Statistical Abstract of the United States, U. S. Department of Commerce, Bureau of the Census, July 1970, p. xiii. 52.8 percent of America's total population is under 30 years of age.
[2]"Campus Tensions and Evangelical Response," by Robert J. Bartel, in *Christianity Today,* June 6, 1969.
[3]"Instant Gratification," Mortimer R. Feinberg, Reprinted

from Family Health, in Success, Inc., December, 1970.

⁴Billy Graham, in "His Business Is the Bible," by Simon Kavanaugh in *Rocky Mountain News* "Festival," December 13, 1970.

⁵"Campus Tensions and Evangelical Response," Robert J. Bartel in *Christianity Today,* June 6, 1969.

⁶Rocky Mountain News "Festival," Sunday, December 13, 1970.

⁷"John Bunyan and the Contemporary Student," E. Beatrice Batson, *Christianity Today,* Sept. 11, 1970.

⁸Ibid.

⁹*ACTION* Editorial, Fall, 1970.

¹⁰"Teenage Manual: Spock Speaks Out on Sex," *The Denver Post,* Wed., Nov. 4, 1970.

¹¹"The Christian Student's Cross" *The Presbyterian Journal,* May 6, 1970.

¹²King Features Syndicate, Inc. 1959.

¹³"Stranded in the Present," Kenneth Keniston, Adolescence for Adult, Blue Cross Assn., 1969.

¹⁴"The Week in Religion," RNS, December 11, 1970.

¹⁵Ibid.

¹⁶"Campus Unrest: Cause/Cure," Reprinted in *Action,* Fall, 1970.

¹⁷*The Presbyterian Journal,* Editorial, January 1, 1969.

5

"People are the root of all problems."

This was one respondent's answer to our survey question, ". . . what do you think is the one important problem people like yourself are concerned about?" 9 percent of those surveyed agreed—7 percent said personal problems are number one.

I read about a man who was learning to drive and had hired an instructor. They took the car to a country road. Within an hour, the student driver was doing very well—stopping, starting, backing up and parking.

Finally, he said to his instructor, "This is easy! Somebody has exaggerated to me the difficult task of learning to drive. There really isn't anything to it."

The instructor then suggested that they go from the quiet country road into the rush-hour traffic. In a few moments, the student driver was wiping the perspiration from his brow. There were cars ahead of him and behind him. Several were honking their horns. Nervously, the learner returned to the country road, where he stopped and said to the instructor, "You know, if it just weren't for the other people!"

And the instructor answered, "Yes, that's about all there is to driving a car—just the other people."

There is more to life than "the other people," but I say that we are involved with other people at almost every "turn of the road," and it is a problem. At least, it is a problem to the majority of people.

But people's *interpretation* of the problem varied extremely. One respondent said: "Lack of involvement! People don't care about what happens to anyone else. Everyone is too self-centered."

Another person responded this way: "Well, people are bothering with too many things that don't concern them. In plain words, they are busybodies!"

When I picked up my Bible to look for the answers to the questions concerning HUMAN RELATIONSHIPS, I was immediately impressed by the fact that the Bible does not evade reality, nor does it shield us from it. There is the admission in Scripture that human relationships will cause us problems.

Getting along with people is not easy: "Don't quarrel with anyone. Be at peace with everyone, just as much as possible" (Romans 12:18, LNT). The Apostle Paul knew that an ideal, perfect situation is non-existent. But we are not responsible for other people's inaction or wrong action—only for our own. So the responsibility for good human relations is mine alone.

Man looks for excuses in the group. He tries to lose personal responsibility in the crowd. He will not say "I am responsible, I am to blame." He generalizes: "People, other people are the problem." But God holds individuals responsible, not groups.

The Authorized Version of Romans 12:18 puts the final responsibility on me. *I* am to do all I can. "If it be possible, as much as lieth in you, live peaceably with all men."

The Bible informs us that we are going to have enemies and then gives a solution to this problem. This solution centers in the greatest of Scripture themes— the theme of love.

"Though I speak with the tongues of men and of angels, and have not love, I am become as sounding brass, or a tinkling cymbal. And though I have the gift of prophecy, and understand all mysteries, and all knowledge; and though I have all faith, so that I could remove mountains, and have not love, I am nothing. And though I bestow all my goods to feed the poor, and though I give my body to be burned, and have not love, it profiteth me nothing. Love suffereth long, and is kind; love envieth not; love vaunteth not itself, is not puffed up, Doth not behave itself unseemly, seeketh not her own, is not easily provoked, thinketh no evil; Rejoiceth not in iniquity, but rejoiceth in the truth; Beareth all things, believeth all things, hopeth all things, endureth all things. Love never faileth" (1 Corinthians 13:1-8).

"This is Christ's eternal message, his most profound teaching. The essence of all religion—the noblest of man's pursuits—is summed up in this simple formula. Having love, you have everything; without love, you are nothing. . . . Love is the gateway through which man must pass to find God. 'Beloved, let us love one another; for love is of God; and he who loves is born of God and knows God. He who does not love does not know God; for God is love' (1 John 4:7-8)."[1]

When a man learns to love as God wants him to love, he is well on his way to finding the answer to his problems.

The Bible informs us that love is essential to human life. That is why God said, "Thou shalt love the Lord thy God with all thy heart, and with all thy soul, and with all thy strength, and with all thy mind; and thy neighbor as thyself" (Luke 10:27). You see,

42

God knows that for a man to be really alive—emotionally, mentally, physically and spiritually—love is essential to that whole man. When He came to demonstrate what God is like, He not only said love yourself, but love your neighbor and love your enemy. He also waits patiently for your "neighbor" and your "enemy" to avail themselves of His Gift of Eternal Life. "God commendeth his love toward us, in that, while we were yet sinners, Christ died for us" (Romans 5:8). How unequalled is God-given love; He proved it with the life of His Son.

"Let love be your greatest aim," said the Apostle Paul in 1 Corinthians 14:1 (LNT). Love is not optional; it is a requisite; it is commanded! The Scripture clearly says, "Thou shalt love the Lord thy God."

The fact that it was a command bothered me. I say that because I immediately realized it was a command which affects the *will* of man. But I was quick to agree. Our will can bend to do anything that God commands us to do. When He tells me to bend my will, my emotions, my strength, and my intellect to loving God, I realize that God would not ask me to do anything I am not capable of doing, or He will not enable me to do it.

What bothered me momentarily was—how can we command love? Love is an emotion. Love does not need to bring the will into play. When a person falls in love, he just *is* in love—it happens automatically. I also asked myself: Who wants to be the victim of a *commanded* love? Then, I had to face the fact that Jesus knows what is in man.

Our emotions are unstable. One moment we are high with great thoughts, and we become noble individuals and register surges of love and compassion. But at other times, we have surges of resentment. The same is true of our emotions toward God. There are days when we really love God; at other times we become resentful and argumentative with God. God is saying that we dare not operate by our emotions alone. Love for God is *more* than emotion, it is love "with all thine heart, with all thy soul, and with all thy might" (Deuteronomy 6:5).

My wife, Betty and I got into a little discussion several months ago after I went home from a hard day of work. I didn't think she was overly sweet on that particular occasion, so I said to her, "Now, you be nice to me. I've preached four times today."

She barked to me, "Well, you be nice to me. I've listened to you four times today."

So, I put on my pajamas, turned some music on the stereo, and stretched out on the carpet in the living room to wait for her to fix me a sandwich and bring it in. A love song was playing so I got sentimental and all wrapped up in the song.

I said, "Hey, Bet, come in."

She was fixing the sandwich and didn't respond quickly. By the time she got into the living room, that song had finished and another one of a completely different tempo was playing on the stereo.

She said, "What was it that you wanted?"

My emotions had changed and I said, "Forget it. I just want my sandwich."

Unfortunately, we ride a roller coaster on our emotional being. God knows this. When God says, "I want you to love me" He wants more than our fickle emotions. He wants our hearts. He says, "You shall love the Lord, thy God, with *all* of your emotions! I want it to be intellectual; I want you to direct your thinking; I want you to get involved with your physical strength, your inward strength, I want you to put your total being into loving me."

Jesus made it clear to His followers: "Your strong love for each other will prove to the world that you are my disciples" (John 13:35, LNT)—Not talk of love, but acts of love.

"Who is my neighbor?" asked a lawyer of Jesus (Luke 10:29). Jesus told him the Good Samaritan story, which he concluded with a question of His own: "Which now of these three, thinkest thou, was neighbor unto him that fell among the thieves? The lawyer rightly deduced: He that shewed mercy on him. And Jesus said to him, Go, and do thou likewise" (Luke 10:36,37).

A neighbor, then, is either someone who is in *need* of help or someone who can *give* that help. He is your neighbor who you know has a need, and you are a neighbor only if you help him. Compassion makes us neighbors, not physical proximity.

But "neighbor" has a broader meaning: "God so loved the *world*." "Neighbor" also means the ". . . new families, families of all races, nationalities, religions, incomes and standards who live within a few blocks of each other and even in the same apartment house . . ."[2]

Our need for involvement with people is interestingly illustrated in the following story:

"I dreamed I had a million dollars and never needed to work again."

"Splendid," said his friend, "but is that all? What was the rest of your dream?"

"Well," he continued, "In my dream I thought of

all the things I could now do with my million bucks. I would have the fanciest food money could buy. I would buy a fine house. Only the sportiest and most expensive automobile would suit me from now on. Clothing? Only the richest and finest would ever cover me again. Oh, I was in clover all right. My fondest wishes had come true."

"Then what happened?" his friend asked.

As he related his dream, it turned into a nightmare. "Listen. I became hungry and went down for some breakfast. There wasn't any. My wife was in tears. The food she had ordered the day before hadn't been delivered. Not even a bottle of milk or the morning newspaper greeted me when I opened the door. I tried to telephone the grocery but the line was dead. I said, 'Oh, well, I'll take a walk and bring back something for breakfast.'

"The street was deserted. Not a bus, streetcar or cab was in sight. I walked on and on. Nothing in sight. Thinking something had happened only to my neighborhood, I decided to go to another, but not even a train was moving. Then people began to appear on the street; first, only a few, then many, then hundreds. I joined them and began asking questions. 'What happened? Where can I buy food?' Then I got a jolt. Somebody said, 'Don't you know? Everybody has a million dollars and nobody has to work any more.'

"At first I was stunned. I thought that somehow a mistake, a ghastly mistake, had been made—but there was no mistake! It was really true. Everyone had a million dollars and thought that work was over for him.

"Then it dawned on me as never before that all of

46

us are dependent upon the rest of us; that, to a small extent at least, my labor had a place in the total welfare of mankind. With an angry shout I tossed to the winds even the thought of a million dollars.

"Then I woke up. My dream was over. The sun was shining, the birds were singing and my wife was rattling the breakfast dishes. I looked out of the window and saw a world of people about their tasks, each contributing a little to my life and living, just as I contribute to theirs. I called to my wife, 'Hurry up with that breakfast, Sweetheart; I want to get to work.'"

It has been said that we live in the age of "dry eyes, hard noses, and cold feet." The "wisdom" of man was revealed when he invented something even more sinister than hate—cold indifference!

"A new commandment I give unto you, That ye love one another; as I have loved you, that ye also love one another. By this shall all men know that ye are my disciples, if ye have love one to another" (John 13:34,35). This is the *wisdom of Christ*; this is the essence of His Gospel—that we "love one another."

To love our fellow man is to have a spirit of goodwill toward God. We need to realize that love is essential to our very being because it is a part of God Himself!

We cannot really love our fellow man unless we love God. God has said, "If a man say, I love God, and hateth his brother, he is a liar . . ." (1 John 4:20). To be antagonistic to our brother and to say at the same time that we love God is pure foolishness! If we want to be alive spiritually, mentally and physically, we must first direct these attributes to

God Himself. Secondly, we must allow God's love to flow through us in order to reach our fellow man.

The house of a very poor family was destroyed by fire. They had a four-year-old boy, who was fascinated by everything that happened! Everybody was so kind. They were given extra clothing, extra help, and extra food—things he had never had as a poor boy. He was sitting on his mother's knee, and he looked up at her and said, "Mommy, don't we have another house to burn?" He liked this kindness. You know, kindness is only love in working clothes.

In his book, *The Humanization of Man,* Ashley Montagu tells about Dr. Fritz Talbot who visited the Children's Clinic in Dusseldorf, Germany, some fifty years ago. Dr. Talbot noticed a plump old woman wandering about the wards with a baby on her hip. Inquiring of the Chief of the Clinic, he was told, "Oh, that's Old Anna. Whenever we have a baby for whom everything we could do has failed, we turn it over to Old Anna. She is always successful. She saves them with love."[3]

The only way we can keep from exhausting our grace toward mankind is to continue to be a channel through which God's love flows. This is a continual and daily process. Unless we constantly keep in mind the source of our ability to love, we will easily be irritated by others.

Someone said, "For thirty years I've been coping with people, but I've run out of cope." I think sometimes we cope with situations until we are "out of cope" and then become irritated. It has been said: "To handle yourself, use your head; to handle others, use your heart." Better yet, let God handle your heart, and instead of self—Jesus. "Not I, but Christ liveth in me." Not human effort, but human yielding to the Divine effort through the human.

Love may be difficult to define, but it is not difficult to discern. Apostle Paul emphasizes the necessity to love. He then spells out the characteristics of love. What an amazing and awesome array of attributes:

Love is patient—exercising the same patience with others that God does with us.

Love is kind—treating all as Jesus treated the woman taken in adultery.

Love is humble—not envious of others or inflated with self.

Love is thoughtful—more aware of its duties than its rights.

Love is forgetful—refusing to keep a record of wrongs received.

Love is enduring—its faith, hope and patience never fail.

You, therefore, can see love's characteristics.

"So I know, Pastor, that this is what I need. It's the answer to the problems of human relationships. But, how do I get this kind of love?"

The old self wants to compete with this Divine Love. There is only one effective way of handling it. "Get rid of SELF—hand it over to Jesus. He tells us to deny ourselves, but it is in favor of another self, even Jesus. He is our new, our everlasting life, our eternal self. Instead of me—Jesus. 'Not I live, but Christ liveth in me.' It is not I that pray, but the Holy Ghost prays in me. It is not I that conquers sin but Christ in me does it all."[4]

By now you may be saying: "I know, Pastor. This is what I need, it's the answer to human relationships, but how do I get this kind of love?"

There are three things I believe one has to do to have love. I pray that the Holy Spirit will burn these truths on my heart as well as on yours. I said my heart, too, because I am interested in being a channel.

The first thing that must be done to make this Divine love become part of us, is to *believe that God loves us.* This is important because my attitude toward God determines my actions toward my fellow men.

If I believe that God is a tyrant going around with a spyglass, looking for my misdeeds, then I will act accordingly. On the other hand, if I believe that my Heavenly Father loves me, that He is interested in me, and that He gives me His grace, then I will live up to His expectations.

Just because He gives me His grace does not mean that He gives me everything I ask for. It seems that in His grace He also withholds some things. He is against that which would hurt me; therefore, He will never compromise with the thing that destroys. His love is not sentimental, weak or sickly; it is a courageous, strong force. He knows there is an enemy. He knows the enemy is out to destroy me. That is why the Scriptures say our God is a Consuming Fire. He consumes that which destroys.

As a young man, Dr. A. J. Cronin was in charge of a small hospital. One evening he performed an emergency operation on a little boy. It was a very delicate operation, and the doctor felt great relief when the little fellow breathed freely after it was over. He gave orders to the young nurse and went home filled with gratitude for the success. Late that night a frantic call came for the doctor. Everything had gone wrong, and the child was in desperate condition. When Dr. Cronin got to the bedside the boy was dead.

The nurse had become frightened and had neglected her duty. Dr. Cronin decided she should not be trusted again, and he wrote a letter to the board of health which would end her career as a nurse. He called her in and read the letter to her. She listened in shame and misery, saying nothing. Finally, Dr. Cronin asked, "Have you nothing to say?" She shook her head. She had no excuse to offer. Then she did speak, and this is what she said, "Give me another chance." He did.

God gave us ten rules to live by. Surely His heart has been grieved as, again and again, we violated them. We stand before Him in shame and misery, condemned without excuse. Not because we deserve it, but because of His infinite mercy, God gives us another chance. "For God so loved the world, that he gave his only begotten Son, that whosoever believeth in him should not perish, but have everlasting life" (John 3:16).

I have to come to grips with the facts that God loves me and God is a God of love. This pulls the barriers down and allows the love of God to flow through me.

The second thing that must be done if I want God's love to fill me is, *obey Him*. Believing is not a passive faith but an active faith. It leads me to show my love to Him through obedience. Forget everything else, but please remember: THE LAW OF LOVE IS OBEDIENCE. To obey is the only way to know the joys and benefits of God's love, given in proportion to obedience to Him. John 14:15 says, "If ye love me, keep my commandments."

Turn to 1 John 3:21-23 and read these words: ". . . we have confidence toward God. And whatsoever we ask, we receive of him, because we keep his commandments, and do those things that are pleasing in his sight. And this is his commandment, that we should believe on the name of his Son Jesus Christ, and love one another." If I believe on Jesus Christ as my Saviour and love my fellow man, when I pray I have confidence that God will hear, and will give me that which I petition.

Aly Wassil, in his book *The Wisdom of Christ,* has this to say: "Each man has within him the power to love, but is often either unaware of this power or unwilling to express it. We must *will* to love.

"But what exactly is this love, how do we discover and cultivate it, how can we practice it? 'By love I do not mean any natural tenderness, which is more or less in people according to their constitution; but I mean a larger principle of the soul, founded in reason and piety, which makes us tender, kind and gentle to all our fellow creatures as creatures of God, and for his sake.' (William Law) 'Learn to look with an equal eye upon all beings, seeing the one self in all,' says the ancient Sanskrit work, Srimad Bhagavatam."[5]

Now we are ready for the third step: *Appropriation and application.*

First, God's love invades us. Then we surrender to it, obey it and reach out to our fellow man.

You may be thinking, "I've always wanted to be a lovable person and be able to get along with others. How can I do it?" You can do it by acts of kindness.

A few weeks ago I was riding with an unsaved man to the downtown area. At two different times he slowed up momentarily to let another car in, and I said, "I commend you for that." He said, "It only took ten seconds, and it makes me feel so good when I do it, I've developed a habit."

It makes us feel good to be kind and considerate, to be loving, to let God's love begin to flow through us as we reach out to our fellow man. When we start doing this, something unusual happens, when we start loving, we are loved in return, and that brings fulfillment.

Developing the body, the mind, the talents and acquiring material things will not bring fulfillment. Selfishness will stop you short of lasting satisfaction.

"Love suffereth long, and is kind; love envieth not . . . seeketh not its own, is not provoked, taketh not account of evil." If you live this kind of love, you will have many loyal friends.

There is always room for improvement, but to improve we must strive. The improvement is gradual. The more you love, the more you improve; and the more you improve, the more you love. And the more you yield to God, the more of His infallible love He will pour into your heart.

Although the *concern for race relations* dropped from number three position (in 1968) to number eleven (in 1971), the problem itself has by no means been solved. Black Evangelist, Tom Skinner, believes: "We are in the midst of a revolution and the black brothers on the street are not playing when they say that unless they get justice they will burn the system."[6]

Since 1964, no less than 250 people have been

killed in riots in the United States. Thousands have been injured as a result of the conflict between the races.[7]

There is a great deal of prejudice on the part of some people toward others of a different skin color. Nobody likes to be accused of being prejudiced and few people are honest enough to admit that they are prejudiced. It may help us to know the dictionary definition of this unwanted word: "A judgment or opinion formed beforehand or without thoughtful examination of the pertinent facts, issues, or arguments; especially, an unfavorable, irrational, biased opinion. Hatred of or dislike for a particular group, race, religion, etc."

I think I understand the feelings and preconceived judgments of these people. I was born down South, though not the "deep South," in the 20's. Although my parents were poor, they taught me honesty and fair play. They even took me to Sunday School, where I was taught to sing a little chorus, along with the rest of the boys and girls.

"Jesus loves the little children,
All the children of the world!
Red and yellow, black and white—
They are precious in His sight,
Jesus loves the little children of the world."

I believed that. I believed it because my Sunday School teacher said so. In public school my teacher explained the meaning of the Declaration of Independence. Later I committed to memory a section of this famous American manifesto:

"When in the course of human events it becomes necessary for one People to dissolve the Political Bands which have connected them with another, and

54

to assume among the Powers of the Earth, the separate and equal Station to which the Laws of Nature and of Nature's God entitled them, a decent Respect to the Opinions of Mankind requires that they should declare the causes which impel them to the Separation.

"We therefore hold these Truths to be self-evident, that all Men are created equal, that they are endowed by their Creator with certain unalienable Rights, that among these are Life, Liberty, and the Pursuit of Happiness . . ."

I believed my teacher's interpretation of this official document. And I was satisfied with her explanation when I asked her why one of my playmates— not white—did not go to my school. Although I accepted my parents' and teacher's explanations as "the right way," I now realize that I did not really understand.

At the age of seventeen I became a Christian and through the generosity of the man who hired me in the J. C. Penney Store, I was able to go to college. My studies in the Bible showed me how to get along with God and man. I noticed that "God so loved the *world*," with no mention of black, yellow or white. "God . . . gave His only begotten Son" for "whosoever."

I saw no mention of color or social status in Matthew 11:28: "Come unto me, all ye that labor and are heavy laden . . ." Jesus did not say, "Inasmuch as you have done it unto the least rich, the least educated or the least white," but He said, "Inasmuch as you have done it not to one of the least of these . . ." (Matthew 25:45).

In my study I read about prejudiced Peter and

how, through the infilling and the inspiration of the Holy Spirit, he finally saw the truth and said, "I see very clearly that the Jews are not God's only favorites!" (Acts 10:34 LNT). We need to pray sincerely that God would give us His evaluation of any and every human being. For although man's prejudiced judgment is often skin deep, God always looks on the heart.

One thing I did not find in the Bible was the origin of skin colors. Nor did I find that any particular race, class or group is under the curse of God, any more than all men are under the disapproval of God because of sin.

In *For Men of Good Will,* most of the questions and clichés about the Negro are discounted, particularly that God made the Negro dark as a curse. "No modern Biblical scholar would subscribe to any such theory."[8] Apostle Paul, under the inspiration of the Holy Spirit, told the Athenians (Acts 17:26) that all men are of one blood. The Living New Testament reads: "He created all the people of the world from one man (Adam) and scattered the nations across the face of the earth." All races have one and the same father. All nations have the same God.

John Howard Griffin learned what it was like to live the life of a Negro by becoming one (his skin changed color through drugs and other special treatment). In *Black Like Me,* where he relates his experiences of 1959-1960, he reveals that in the Deep South, many judge on the basis of skin color: ". . . many sincerely think the Negro, because of his very Negro-ness, could not possibly measure up to white standards in work performance. I read recently where one of them said that equality of education and job opportunity would be an even greater tragedy for us. He said it would quickly prove to us that we can't measure up—disillusion us by showing us that we are, in fact, inferior."⁹

After finishing school, I traveled around the world and made another discovery. In the southern part of India I came across the results of the work of Apostle Thomas—first missionary to India. He loved those people of a different color skin, and he gave his life for them.

In China I found the footprints of such men as David Hill and Hudson Taylor. These men loved a lost world and people of every color, because they believed God's Word.

In Africa, David Livingstone's love for the black people is alive today. At home and abroad, there are those who have taken to heart the words of the Apostle of Love (1 John 3:18): ". . . let us not love in word, neither in tongue; but in deed and in truth." Ours is to love all, for all are equal.

At the end of the round-the-world trip, I read the biblical account of a man called Philip (Acts 8). He was in the middle of a tremendous spiritual awakening among people of his own color. Then the Holy Spirit said to Philip, "I'm sending you on a secret assignment down to the Gaza Strip." It was so secret that no one knows how he got there and how he managed to locate the chariot of Ethiopia's Secretary of the Treasury. But there is a clue in verse 39: ". . . the Spirit of the Lord caught away Philip. . . . but Philip was found at Azotus . . ." (50 miles south of Caesarea). That was the return trip. Philip was privileged to experience a mode of transportation that belongs to the future and is really "I. T."—Instant Travel.

The black Ethiopian had obviously made a rest stop, Philip ran thither to him, v. 30 and was reading —at that moment—the 53rd Chapter of Isaiah. Philip followed the Holy Spirit's instructions, explained the Scriptures to the eunuch, "preached unto him Jesus," and baptised him. There were no reservations, no barriers, no aloofness, no differences. The black man got the same treatment as the people back in Samaria.

This same Ethiopian went back to his country, not to overthrow the establishment, change the environment or campaign for social justice. He did something better: he helped change people's hearts. Like Sam Dalton and Tom Skinner, this first-century African went beyond mandatory group action; he sought his soul's freedom first.

Skinner believes: "We must go one step beyond. There's a point where legislation cannot change the human heart. There is a point where social action cannot erase bigotry and hate. Christ has given me true dignity. All I know is that Christ is alive and in me, and because he is living in me, the love of God is actually springing up within my soul . . . it doesn't make any difference to me if society doesn't love me. I am being loved."[10]

Sam Dalton states: ". . . as a Negro seeking not sympathy . . . I believe that the Lord Jesus Christ . . . is the only answer for whatever the dilemma. I am convinced that trusting in Him will do what men, methods and means have thus far and shall continue to fail in achieving . . ."[11]

The trip around the world ended. I began to preach 1 John 3:18 "Let us not love in word, neither in tongue; but in deed and in truth." Although I recalled my childhood prejudices, I now had picked up some facts. I also had picked up another fact: I had no more prejudices; I had learned to love all the people of the world.

Two things helped me to come to grips with my childhood prejudices: The Bible and the Declaration of Independence. If the Scriptures teach anything, they teach that God treats all men alike. He shows no partiality. Was I going to follow my childhood prejudices, or was I going to look realistically at the teaching of the Scriptures? When I studied the Declaration of Independence, I knew that I had to take a stand. It wouldn't be easy.

We cannot legislate or impose equality. There is no simple or easy way to fulfill this great task. But I believe Christ's way is the best way.

I now try to look at the question of equality as an adult and want to be influenced by no one except the teachings of Jesus. Part of our problem is that we interpret the Scriptures to suit our personal views. "Both read the same Bible and pray to the same God, and each invokes His aid against the other. It may seem strange that any man should dare to ask a just God's assistance in wringing their bread from the sweat of other men's faces, but let us judge not, that we be not judged. The prayers of both could not be answered. That of neither has been answered fully. The Almighty has His own purposes. Woe unto the world because of offenses; for it must needs be that offenses come, but woe to that man by whom the offense cometh."[12]

Neither the Scriptures nor the Declaration of Independence convey the idea that men are created equal, physically. Jim Ryun can run a mile in four minutes. Unless I improve rapidly, I probably never will.

The Bible does not teach that men are created equal mentally or intellectually. The Scriptures have no quarrel with the results of the I.Q. Tests.

Neither is there equality when it comes to plain common sense. Some people seem to have more than others—like the fellow who worked at a plant where everybody (100 percent) had to sign up, in order to get the insurance policy. Everyone but Fred signed up. Everybody begged Fred to join but he refused. All kinds of high pressure tactics were used, and without success. Finally, the boss, seeing that everyone was going to suffer because of Fred's lack of cooperation, called him in. Hitting the desk with his big hand, the boss stated: "Fred, I want you to sign up right now or you're fired!"

"Hand me the pen," said Fred, and he signed without any hesitation.

The boss scratched his head and asked: "Why were you holding out before?"

"Boss, I ain't had it explained in such a clear, common-sense way before," said Fred.

Nor are we equal when it comes to moral character. Moral equality is an impossibility. I think it was Shakespeare who said that if two men ride a horse, one must ride behind. Some people are behind when it comes to various phases of life. They do not have the physical stamina or they do not have the mental sharpness.

But of this I am convinced: We are all equal before God, because God shows no partiality. This is something the general public needs to come to grips with: apart from God, there is no human equality.

I will go a step further. If you were to look at the subject of equality purely from a humanistic point of view, then the Declaration of Independence is nonsense. But if God is the Creator of all men, then it makes profound sense. Because all men are equal (and therefore equally accountable to God), He is the God of all: the proud, the humble, the good, the bad, the weak and the strong. It is only this context that gives the Declaration of Independence its profound sense and meaning.

The "Babel sound" of the "give and take" of equal rights has brought us no closer to a solution. We have left the most important element—God—out of our labors. There is nothing right about Civil Rights until the heart is right.

Everyone has a right to equal learning. Many thought that the Civil Rights Act of 1964 would solve our race issue. What has happened since then shows that we need something more radical than legislation. "We need legislation to regulate us in many areas of our lives, but unless the heart is reached there will be no basic solution. That is why it is so important that a great spiritual awakening come to America, so that men will love their neighbor as themselves."[13]

Everyone has a right to equal treatment, equal justice, equal voting privileges, equal liberty. This puts a tremendous responsibility upon all of us. God has blessed America because, as the "melting-pot" of the world, we have not tried to produce a super-strain or a pure race. We are sinners all, "For all have sinned, and come short of the glory of God" (Romans 3:23). First must come a genuine reconciliation with our Maker, and then we will be capable of seeing our neighbor as God sees him.

As a Christian, I look past the skin, "Man looketh on the outward appearance, but the Lord looketh on the heart" (1 Samuel 16:7). You see, the heart stands for the moral, the spiritual, and the intellectual life of the man. John Howard Griffin tells how an aging Negro man in Mobile, Alabama, interprets his responsibility to God: " 'They're God's children (the white race), just like us . . . even if they don't act very godlike any more. God tells us straight—we've got to love them, no *ifs, ands* and *buts* about it. Why, if we hated them, we'd be sunk down to their level. There's plenty of us doing just that, too. . . . you can't get around what's right, though . . . when we stop loving them, that's when they win.' "[4]

The call to Christ is heard across America. Our only hope is in Him, for He has shown us The Way of self-denial and of active love.

There is a verse of Scripture in Jeremiah, Chapter 13, which questions whether or not the individual can change the color of his skin. It is amazing how many of us, with the help of the sun, want to become darker, while some dark people wish they were white. We could use a dose of Apostle Paul's philosophy: "I have learned, in whatsoever state I am, therewith to be content."

God is interested in the heart. While the Ethiopian could not change his skin, he could have his heart changed. That is the glory of the gospel. That is the story of Philip. He did not preach a sermon on social responsibilities. He did not preach about the tyranny of Rome, or about the race problem, or about slavery. I read one beautiful phrase here—that Philip preached unto the Ethiopian: *Jesus!* Do you know why? Because Jesus is the only One who can change the heart. It is an amazing thing when the heart is changed—it doesn't matter about the skin!

We will spend, and send whites to win blacks across the ocean, but it has well been said that "Charity begins at home." And what good will it do me to tell a "black" that God loves him if he's not convinced that this "white" loves him?

What is the answer? Integration? Separation? Legislation? Revolution? Jesus told Nicodemus clearly and plainly: "You must be born again."

[1]Aly Wassil, *The Wisdom of Christ* (New York: Evanston, and London: Harper & Row Publishers) p. 6.

[2]Mary Davis Gillies, "How to Get Acquainted—The Neighbors," *How to Keep House* (New York: Harper & Brothers Publishers) pp. 44-45.

[3]"Target Theology," January 1969 Sermon by Dr. William E. Everheart, Springfield, Missouri.

[4]*Eternity Magazine.*

[5]Aly Wassil, *The Wisdom of Christ* (New York, Evanston, and London: Harper & Row, Publishers).

[6]Tom Skinner, "Evangelicals and the Black Revolution," *Christianity Today* (April 10, 1970), p. 10.

[7]Statistical Abstracts, Department of Commerce Publications, 91st Volume, 1970.

[8]John Howard Griffin, *Black Like Me* (Houghton Mifflin Company, Boston, 1961), p. 144.

[9]Ibid.

[10]Tom Skinner, *Black and Free* (Zondervan Publishing House, Grand Rapids, Mich. 1968) p. 151.

[11]Sam Dalton, "Sin Not Skin" (Denver, Colo.).

[12]Glenn R. Capp of Baylor University, *Famous Speeches In American History* (Bobbs-Merrill Company, Ins.).

[13]Billy Graham, "God and the Color of Man's Skin," *Decision* (August, 1965) p. 14.

[14]Op. cit., *Black Like Me,* p. 103.

6

"The drug traffic is too heavy."

Have an aspirin! It will give you pain relief. It's a drug. But then, so is tea and coffee, tobacco and liquor. Caffeine is a stimulant, alcohol and nicotine are depressants.

When we are on either sleeping pills, tranquilizers, sedatives, diet pills, stay awake pills or pep pills, we are on drugs. Here we also will find barbiturates, phenobarbital, Thorazine, hydrochloride, Dexadrine and amphetamines—all legal, all helpful drugs. Yet only 6 percent of those surveyed considered drugs our number one problem.

Many a child started his drug trip beginning at the family medicine cabinet. He could get high on amphetamines (diet, pep and stay awake pills), and he could come down with barbiturates (sedatives and tranquilizers).

The time is long past due when we should stop moralizing, preaching and scaring on the subject of drugs. Now we need to be knowledgeable, objective and honest. It would help if we would begin with ourselves. Let's be sure that we do not judge our actions and the actions of others by different standards.

If we do not want our society destroyed by drug abuse, we are going to have to make mental, educational and practical changes. At the moment, the average adult is not in a position to speak convincingly about drug abuse.

"The average respectable adult consumes three to five mind-altering drugs a day, beginning with the stimulant caffeine in coffee or tea, proceeding from there to nicotine and alcohol, often a tranquilizer, not uncommonly a sleeping pill at night, and sometimes an amphetamine the next morning to overcome the effects of the sedative taken the night before."[1]

And still the nationwide advertising campaign goes on. "Attitudes conducive to drug use are communicated by commercials for tranquilizers, pep pills, sleeping pills, and weight-reducing pills. These advertisements help to teach that when an individual has a physical pain or personal problem, he should swallow a pill, take a drink, or smoke a cigarette."[2]

Why do young people refuse to take seriously the efforts of adults to explain the dangers of marijuana? Are these same parents also willing to talk about alcohol and tobacco? ". . . reports indicate that 95 to 100 percent of the heroin addicts actually started with alcohol and tobacco illegally in their early teens."[3]

At present, we are doing more harm than good in our fight against drug abuse, not only because we have a double standard, but also because of an unfair and unrealistic penalty system.

The situation is not helped where marijuana is classified as a narcotic and considered to be a felony, while use of LSD (a far more dangerous drug) is only a misdemeanor. Furthermore, legislation—"for" or "against"—cannot solve the problem of drug abuse. "The absurdity of pretending to solve the problem by passing a law against it, while ignoring the complex social and psychological reasons for drug use, is illustrated by the enormous range of noncontrolled substances that people can use to alter their consciousness including banana peel, glue, floor wax, nutmeg, gasoline, catnip, freon gas."[4]

Why do we have a drug problem in the first place? What is behind the drug use and abuse of our children? Some feel that it is part of our cultural philosophy. Part of the drug problem is just plain ignorance. How many adults know that going off phenobarbital is more dangerous than stopping the use of either alcohol, heroin or morphine? As it stands now, neither parents nor teachers or even doctors have enough knowledge about drugs.

The drug age is probably here to stay, so we owe it to ourselves to be well informed on the subject. Since drug use is linked to psychological and emotional conditions, we will probably have to make it part of the school curriculum, starting early.

"Beset with anxiety, frustration, fear of failure, inner conflict and doubts, the adolescent may find that amphetamines and marijuana promote conversation and friendship, barbiturates loosen inhibitions, hallucinogens heighten sensations, and narcotics provide relief and escape. Drug use may also signify deeper personal problems . . . If these boys and girls have been unable to gain affection, acceptance and approval at home, they can, through drugs, be very effective in bringing their parents and others closer, gaining a perverse form of attention if nothing else."[5]

One twelve-year-old girl won a newspaper essay contest by advocating heavy doses of LSD for young people today. She said: "What the kids of today need is lots of LSD—Love, Security, and Discipline."[6]

The reasons for drug use among young people vary with the individual.

"Graham Blaine, chief of psychiatry in the Student Health Services at Harvard University, has summarized some of the forces that influence boys and girls of junior high and high school age in this direction. They may take drugs to:

1. prove their courage by indulging in risk-taking,
2. act out their rebellion and hostility toward authority.
3. facilitate sexual desires and performance,
4. elevate themselves from loneliness and provide an emotional experience, or
5. attempt to find the meaning of life."[7]

Youngsters and adults alike need a power greater than themselves. Every time they reach for a cigarette, a liquor glass or a pill, they are saying: "I can't make it on my own." And they are right. But this is why we should reach out for God. He is, and He has, what is missing in us.

Happiness is everyone's pursuit. But nothing in the world can give lasting, satisfying joy like Jesus can. Everything else is a mirage. Drugs don't really solve anything for very long, if at all. Only an encounter with Christ brings reality, meaning and truth.

" 'When you go up on acid, there's always that terrible coming down again. With Jesus, you just keep going up, gradually and surely. You keep growing and learning step by step how to meet and overcome your difficulties. There are problems with self-discipline, of course, but joy and fulfillment all the way.' "[8]

The "Jesus People" are proving that the indwelling Spirit of Christ has the ability and the power to take care of our personal and social hangups. ". . . total commitment to Jesus Christ as Lord and Master has brought me the full deliverance which I had been seeking from my past problems, and daily rich spiritual experiences far surpassing in beauty and reality the counterfeit experiences of LSD."[9]

Jesus promised us an abundant life, here and now —"satisfaction guaranteed." As a special bonus, we are born into the great big wonderful family of God. Just think how wonderful it would be if all of the professing Christians would really get "hooked" on Christ and then become Jesus "pushers!"

[1]Senator Harold E. Hughes (Chairman of the Senate Subcommittee on Alcoholism and Narcotics), IDEA Report on National Conference of Drug Abuse, 1969, p. 5.
[2]Ibid, p. 8.
[3]Ibid, p. 8.
[4]Ibid.
[5]Op. cit., IDEA Report, pp. 13, 14.
[6]From "The Log." published by Haven of Rest, Hollywood, Cal. Vol. 37, No. 3.
[7]Dr. Sprague W. Hazard, "Drug Abuse In Adolescence" (Position Statement of the American Academy of Pediatrics Committee on Youth), IDEA Report.
[8]Jeff, a former drug addict, quoted by Catherine Marshall in "An Answer to Drugs," *Guideposts,* May 1970.
[9]Lambert Dolphin (assistant manager of the Radio Physics Laboratory, Stanford Research Institute, Palo Alto, Cal.), quoted by Dr. William E. Everheart in "A Trip to LSD Land," January 14, 1968.

7

"Government is degenerating."

Can you think of at least one well-known nation that is not hamstrung by one or more major crises, be they political, economical, moral or social?

Look down to South America or across to Africa, Europe and the Middle East. Look over to Asia and the Orient. Everywhere, governments are in serious trouble.

Even the U.S.A., the envy of so many other nations is crippled by an unbelievable national debt, by onerous taxes, by seemingly uncontrolled crime, by drug and sex abuse. Among those surveyed, 6 percent considered government the number one problem. Jesus spoke of the coming "distress of nations." It has come.

"Government" is a Bible word. Government is a Divine concept. Government is a good idea. We need law and order. We need organization and authority.

But today, Americans are concerned that government controls are out of control. They are perplexed by the abuse of power in high places. They object to congressional high living, supported by high taxes. They dislike excessive waste and welfare and resent the gradual loss of rights and freedoms.

Our constitution is being emasculated by interpretations of jurists and is being ridiculed by citizens. Consequently, our moral superstructure is dangerously weakened. Somehow, government of, by and for the people, is beginning to sound like a philosophy from another planet. Is it any wonder that many are disillusioned and think that there is no plan or purpose to life? Should it surprise us that so many people seem to be hypnotized by a death wish?

Are power-crazed governments wiring us for self-destruction? Must we sacrifice ourselves on the altar of the god of political science? Is some demonic force instigating nation against nation? Why can't we come to some agreement at the peace tables? Are we fighting a losing battle for peace, at home and abroad? These are the questions that are torturing men's minds today.

Some feel that, internally and externally, mankind is faced with too formidable a foe. Man's moral nature is too corrupt and his physical body too weak to withstand the seemingly inevitable process of annihilation.

More criminals walk the streets than are behind bars. Almost anyone's integrity can be bought. There are never enough hospitals to house the diseased and dying. And after you're dead, you are forgotten. Life has no meaning or purpose, so some say.

We said that "government" is a Scripturally-oriented word. Government is a divine institution; therefore, government without God cannot succeed. Taking God out of government is like removing the brain from the body. Government minus God equals chaos.

God did not turn man loose on this planet without principles and guidelines. God does everything "decently and in order." God proceeds with a purpose and a plan. He is vitally concerned with His world and needs to be involved in the affairs of men.

But man rejected God. God foresaw the floundering and eventual failure of godless government. Isaiah 9:6 and 7 will come to pass. Good government will come, of which "there shall be no end." And God Himself will be the government.

There can be no two ways about government. It must be either God's good way or man's suicidal way. God and government, like love and marriage, go together. You can't have one without the other.

We can try to make our own way in the darkness of the unknown, or we can choose to proceed confidently in the light of Divine direction. Either we are an important part of a Master Plan, or we are driftwood on a senseless sea; it cannot be both, or even part of both. When it comes to theists and atheists, there can be no philosophical composite. Either I am an accident of nature, or I am an invention of God. If I cannot be sure on this point, then I cannot be sure about anything.

Maybe we need a flashback to where it all started —in Eden. While God gave Adam governing powers over the animal and over the natural world, He also laid down the law to Adam himself. At one point, when Divine plans and purposes were sufficiently frustrated by man's disregard and disobedience of God's rules and regulations, the Lord had to start all over again, using Noah's family.

Again God gave guidelines. This should make it clear that our Creator has definite intentions for mankind, both on personal and on social levels.

Under Nimrod, a political confederacy was formed, not under God but in open defiance against God. Nimrod gained control on earth by armed force and was the progenitor of all the Alexanders, Napoleons and Hitlers. When a man rebels against his Maker, he will invariably abuse his God-given authority. The confusion of Babel is repeated every time a nation leaves God out of government.

Later, God chose a man by the name of Abraham to bring into being a nation that would be separate from the nations of the world, in the sense that they would worship the true and living God. The people of Israel were not favorites, but servants. Whenever they acted like God's favorites, they became intolerable and suffered the judgment of God.

Choosing this nation was part of God's long-range plan. That plan was to bring a redeemer into this world and restore man's position with God. For man to reign, man must be restored.

Thus, Isaiah promised that a virgin would conceive, the Savior would be born, and the kingdoms of this world would become His. In the fullness of time He came, lived about 33 years in complete obedience to the will of God, voluntarily died to provide eternal life for all mankind, and was raised from death to life through the power of God. Presently, He is serving as our advocate in heaven and promises to return to establish the Kingdom Age on earth.

Now, as it was in the beginning and throughout the history of the human race, man tries to run things without God. But it's no good without God. Welfare, high taxes and tension are direct results of man trying to go his own direction, rather than going God's way. Some of the best brains and hearts are giving themselves to establish peace on earth. But there will be no peace until His will is done on earth as it is done in heaven.

While I agree that there is much social disorder on

earth, there is also much evidence of law and order in the natural and spiritual world. Many scientists tell us that everything in the universe testifies of the existence of God. Mathematical precision alone, in the substance and laws of nature, should sufficiently prove the existence of a rational design.

Trace the course of events, and you will see at work the immutable moral law of God. Where there was moral apostasy there was national decay. Where there was obedience there was blessing.

When Christ came on the mortal scene, Israel— the chosen nation—was in a state of dispersion and oppression. They were a people without a country, precisely because they had disobeyed God's laws. All this had been spelled out to them in detail when they first occupied the Promised Land.

Government will always degenerate whenever God is disregarded. We cannot have good government without God's moral and spiritual guidelines. We cannot hope to have a healthy economy unless we are willing to put God's will in first place.

Greed and graft come on the wake of moral decline. Immorality increases as the fear of the Lord decreases. God-fearing government is made up of God-fearing individuals. Things don't just happen. Everything is subject to the law of cause and effect. We are experiencing "the distress of nations" simply because we have ignored the Divine rules and regulations that were given for our direction and protection. "All we like sheep have gone astray; we have turned every one to his own way" (Isaiah 53:6). And some have even turned to Satan's way. But— our own or Satan's—both ways lead to definite disaster.

God gave us guidelines for good reason. His laws are not an afterthought; His rules are not superfluous; His commands are not superficial; nor are His demands optional. Yet His "yoke is not grievous."

There is the law of sowing and reaping. Every man shall receive accordingly. God does not operate accidentally. There will be no mix-ups and no mistakes. There will be no breach of justice. Perhaps sooner than we would like to think, obedience will receive its reward and disobedience will receive its punishment.

But we are getting ahead of ourselves. It is Divinely predicted that "The Man of Sin" will become an economic and military genius, for he will be endowed with supernatural, satanic power. Many of the nations will be waiting for him, because they themselves will have failed to bring about peace and prosperity. Having rejected God's good government, they will be forced to accept Satan's evil government.

Such a development will only confirm Apostle Paul's statement that man was created to be a follower, and specifically, a follower of God. But he is a follower. If he fails to follow Good, he will only follow Evil—his own or Satan's.

So, good leadership is dependent upon good "followership." Good government is dependent upon God.

8

"Barring a moral renaissance, we've had it."

". . . every man did that which was right in his own eyes" (Judges 17:6).

Item: A Protestant denomination supports Black Panthers and radicals; encourages deception, power manipulation, civil disobedience, violence and drug use, accepts the homosexual as normal.[1]

Item: Ministers of another denomination "propose that married men make themselves available to lonely single women."[2]

Item: A "devout" nude couple publicly partakes of Holy Communion with the approval of pastors of a third denomination.[3]

A friend of mine used to be a sound sleeper. Now he tosses and turns all night. He's thinking seriously of getting out of the insurance business because of the deceptive, unethical practices of his superiors. Prior to his present job, he had been a career army man but left because of the wholesale dishonesty, not only in his department but generally. Integrity is a rare bird that is on the verge of extinction on the American moral scene. Yet only 6 percent of those surveyed considered morality the number one problem.

But even the average Christian does not relate to the church or the Bible in moral decisions. In matters of divorce, adultery, remarriage, abortion, sexual perversion and pornography, the courts and the government are expected to pass final judgment.

The liberal church, in its efforts to lose the arbitrary, dogmatic and authoritative image, has swung to the other extreme. Even when the broadminded ministers have been saying no more than, "Folks, it's up to you," the folks have interpreted it to mean, "It's OK to do everything."

People, however, insist on being told what to do. They do not want to be told to do as they please. They don't want the responsibility that goes with it. People have their own reasons and motives for wanting someone else to make the decisions. They still may not do it, but they do want to know what they are, or are not, supposed to do. But when it comes to legislating morality, it cannot be done, because morality is not so much a matter of conduct as of character. People cannot be forced to be moral. Even Jesus said, "You shall know the truth, and the truth will make you free." He did not force people to accept the truth—only to know it.

Legislation having to do with the control of overt moral action is necessary in the present society; but, at best, it is a stopgap maneuver. Human nature will not change until it receives God's new morality within the heart, which works from the inside out. And until a man experiences this moral renewal, he will always find ways of getting around legislated laws.

God respects individuality. He would have us do His will only if we want to. He will use me only if I let Him. People, on the other hand, resort to every trick in the bag. They will use inexhaustible methods to influence and control one another. They will make unfair and underhanded appeals. They will use heavy-handed threats. But God tells it like it is. He lays it on the line. He makes the proposition and invites us to accept or reject it.

It is worse than useless for the church to intimidate people. Some of us have tried to improve on God's approach to mankind. Our words and actions imply that God didn't go far enough. Instead of attracting people to the Lord, we have tried to scare them out of hell and consequently frightened them away from heaven.

We have applied our "know so" position to every other area of religious experience—to areas where we had no authority to be dogmatic. People saw through it and lost faith.

In too many instances we have taken the faithful few and inadvertently made highly-trained hypocrites out of them, when we should have been developing saints. We've been high on Bible knowledge and low on spiritual performance. We've graduated expert hairsplitters, when we should have been specializing in peacemakers. We have become proficient at "straining gnats and swallowing camels."

We've defended the faith over and beyond the call of duty and to the extent that we've isolated ourselves from friend and foe alike. We've been fighting sinners instead of sin. We loved our church, our organization, more than we loved souls.

We split because we were carnal and we merged because we were weak. Perhaps it's just as well. Maybe it would be good for the established, institutionalized church to experience a catastrophic persecution. Out of the fire and ashes could emerge a vital handful, similar to the one that turned the first-century world upside down. The best thing that happened to the cosy Christian communal center at

Jerusalem was when they were dispersed to the ends of the then-known world.

Why this exposé of the state of professing Christianity when we are supposedly talking about the general moral decline and not about religion? It is because I believe that by default, we may have been a primary contributor to America's moral decline.

When I, as a Christian, am unethical myself, I am doing at least three things: 1) I am being a hypocrite; 2) I am not deterring immorality, and 3) I am contributing to the growth of immorality. Only when I am genuinely and actively ethical, only then, am I effective against moral decline.

Quite a few clergymen have been questioning the morality of war. Some have marched in its protest. More is said about war and peace in another chapter, but I would like to protest a war that is closer to home. I am talking about the over 1,000 red-blooded Americans who are massacred—each week—by the mechanical missile, the automobile. That's one auto fatality every ten minutes, not counting the seriously injured, the permanently crippled, the material damage and the mental anguish. I am talking about the moral responsibility of the driver who exceeded the speed limit, the driver who was hostile and inconsiderate and the driver who was just plain careless with human life. I am protesting because *more than half* of these auto fatalities are alcohol-related.

If the drinking driver has a right to drive on the same street with the non-drinker, then the latter has just forfeited *his* rights. If the intoxicated driver has a right to drive, then make him fully responsible for his driving and his drinking. If we talk about rights, let's have some real rights for the non-drinking driver.

Currently, there is considerable discussion about extending the segregation to the smoker and the non-smoker on public transportation and in public establishments. I am in favor of this move because, under the present arrangement, the non-smoker is non-existent—unless he's holding his breath.

I am not suggesting segregated driving facilities for drinkers and non-drinkers. I am simply pointing out how the selfish, thoughtless few have been permitted to take advantage of the many.

To say that the drinking driver is not responsible at the time of the accident is to miss the point. Responsibility is not limited to one point in time. By way of comparison, let us say that a man is being tried for setting off a bomb. At the time of the explosion, the guilty person may have been nowhere in the vicinity; he may have crossed a state line. Furthermore, the blast occurred several hours after the timer was triggered. The man is not being tried because there was a blast, but because several hours earlier this person placed and triggered a bomb.

Is the human consumption of alcohol any less a triggered time bomb? I say it is not. Last year alcohol caused 24,000 deaths by auto, not to mention other alcohol-related deaths and injuries.

Regardless of how irresponsible a drinking person becomes, he is responsible for taking the drink in the first place. The Bible supports this concept. The drunkard (no special category for the alcoholic) is listed along with sex perverts, swindlers, robbers, thieves, perjurers, and holds each one fully responsible for his actions. (See 1 Corinthians 5:11; 6:10).

Many modern doctors, psychologists and jurists take this same position. They would not be working with the neurotic, the addict and the alcoholic if they did not believe in the moral responsibility of these people.

Apostle Paul used to say, "I will not be brought under the power of any" (1 Corinthians 6:12). What then is the alcoholic's answer? It is this: "I will not put myself under the power of alcohol." The only way to do this is not to take the first drink.

"But I have no power over it!" Then keep your distance. The way not to yield to temptation is to keep away from the tempting situation.

And now we have the highly publicized and popularized "situational ethics." And what an impossible situation we are in! The people who scoffed at God's wise, protective laws for man are now understandably humiliated. However, there are still some promoters of "situational ethics" who preach the maxim that "love is absolute."

Let us briefly analyze this concept. We will soon realize that this statement, "love is absolute," has no meaning when divorced from the intellect and the will. Love, to be meaningful, is dependent upon the mind and the volition to give it definition, interpretation, embodiment, direction and expression. In other words, love is inoperative without rational guidelines.

"Situational ethics" says love is absolute. But if our love is dependent upon our thinking, then our mind must conceive love, develop it, interpret it. Man's mind must decide what love is and what it is not.

Can a man's mind be absolute? Remember that an absolute never changes; it has no need to change. If it does change, it is not an absolute. An absolute is fundamental; it is the ultimate.

Take any ten men and you will have ten differing "absolutes." Not only this, but man's mind is full of inconsistencies and contradictions. Knowing all this we still want to be our own little absolute gods. By doing so we assume impossible responsibilities. We must write all of our own rules as we go. In every new situation we must make new decisions. Experience proves that we are incapable of living up to such responsibility.

No child and no teen-ager is capable of handling this awesome assignment properly and satisfactorily. Anyone who says he can, is fooling no one but himself. Our young people lack the facts, the wisdom and the experience. They admit it. They beg for solid values. They cannot cope with life without definite guidelines. But when they see adults fumbling and floundering, their despair is complete. They are assailed by frustrations and inner doubts.

What develops in a situational ethics-orientated society? Since everybody can't be right, somebody has to be proven wrong. In the confusion and chaos, the clever and the strong-willed—the peers—will call the shots and formulate the life-style, right or wrong. They will dictate the definition of "love"—or whatever motivating power is in vogue. Norms and standards will be instituted. Next comes organization, which automatically takes us the full cycle to "the establishment." This is what happens when men become wise in their own eyes and reject God's absolutes. A man is forced to accept another man's poor excuse for the absolute. Scoff at God's wisdom and settle for man's foolishness.

Is love rational; can love think—independently? When I decide on a certain course of action, is it because love has spoken, or is it because I rationalized and willed in the name of love?

There is a rational Love, but it is not human; it is superhuman and it is Divine. God is love; God and His love are one and the same thing. Yes, love is absolute. But whose love are we talking about—ours or God's? By all means be filled with the love of God and you will be guided by Absolute Love. The immediate results will prove it.

In the final analysis, "situational ethics" is a glaring contradiction because it teaches that there are no absolutes. It is nothing more than so much double-talk. The only thing "situational ethics" teaches for sure is that nothing is sure: no absolutes, no rules, no regulations, no norms, no light, no direction, no assurance, no security—man is adrift, with no sail and no rudder. Is this what we offer our offspring?

But Jesus came, saying, "I am the light of the world. I am the way, the truth and the life." He is the key and the absolute answer. He is the immovable point of reference. He is "the same yesterday, today and forever."

While "situational ethics" have been influencing a large segment of our society, a diabolical philosophical campaign has been in progress, deceiving even "the elect." For two decades the mass media have been promoting a materialistic way of life: Consumption! Self-indulgence! Instant gratification! Self-denial is no longer a virtue. If you want it, get it, take it now, and you're anti-American if you don't.

Who has been setting our economic and moral standards? Certainly not the Bible. National advertising is the New American Bible.

God says sex is sacred. We say, "What's so sacred

about sex?" And we proceed to dissect sex to prove God wrong. After our lab test, we conclude that God, after all, knew what He was talking about; but, of course, we desecrated it in the meantime.

God says a man will reap what he sows. We say: "Maybe it used to be so, but in our technological age we can change all that." So we proceed to write our own ticket which, at this very moment, is propelling us toward national moral bankruptcy. As we fishtail out of control, the thought flashes across our bewildered minds that maybe God was right after all.

Man makes a mousetrap and encloses directions for use. He runs an automobile off the assembly line and provides a maintenance manual. Man builds a simple computer and employs a maintenance engineer, a systems analyst and a programmer. But man wants none of this for himself, even though he needs it most. Man creates only gadgets and equipment, but he, himself, is a complex free moral agent, created in God's likeness.

And God gave man a Guidebook. But because of man's superior (?) wisdom, he self-confidently threw away the Living Manual. He has been in deep trouble ever since. "The world by wisdom knew not God" (1 Corinthians 1:21).

When the Bible isn't read at home or taught in church, the human being does what no computer can do: He begins to make up his own rules and regulations. But his heart is naturally pulled down in the direction of sin. When he is confronted with an ethical decision, he invariably makes the wrong choice. In his mind he finds it simple to justify greed, theft, fraud, immorality. The invented, created one, writes his own rules—hardly a realistic way of operating.

It is not surprising that the family is deteriorating and disintegrating. The parents are too busy for the children and vice versa. As the lines of communication break down, the kids get their values from television, school and their peers.

Our children don't learn from history because they don't believe in it. And anyway, who has time for history when we can't keep up with current events? Who wants to study the past when we cannot comprehend the present? There is just too much to learn.

But I do not think we have a plurality of problems. The problems are symptoms of one basic deficiency. Neither affluence nor knowledge, neither science nor technology can correct this fatal flaw. We are, by nature, morally corrupt. The basic problem of the individual is *moral*. The basic problem of government, race, crime and even pollution is *moral*. Our morality is our vulnerable Achilles' heel.

Why not swallow our stubborn pride and study the Instruction Book? It is not too late to take seriously the note of caution found in an instruction manual: "Before you do it your way, try doing it our way." Our Creator also cautions us: "There is a way which seemeth right unto a man, but the end thereof are the ways of death" (Proverbs 14:12).

King David speaks from experience as he says: "Oh how love I thy law! it is my meditation all the day. Thou through thy commandments hast made me wiser than mine enemies: for they are ever with me. I have more understanding than all my teachers; for thy testimonies are my meditation. I understand more than the ancients, because I keep thy precepts. I have refrained my feet from every evil way, that I might keep thy word. I have not departed from thy judgments: for thou hast taught me. How sweet are thy words unto my taste! yea, sweeter than honey to my mouth! Through thy precepts I get understanding: therefore I hate every false way. Thy word is a lamp unto my feet, and a light unto my path" (Psalms 119:97-105).

The ancient Bible is always contemporary. Its accuracy defies correction. It is changeless Truth in an ever-changing world. Is it too difficult to admit that the Bible's superior philosophy is beyond our human comprehension? Let's not condemn it just because we cannot, or will not, understand it.

We claim to be knowledgeable and intellectual. If we really are, why not put the Word of God to the test? The Bible clearly presents unchanging good, unchanging right and unchanging truth.

The Creator of the universe challenges us to investigate Him, to test His advertising and to prove His product. (See Psalms 34:8; Jeremiah 33:3, Malachi 3:10; Matthew 11:28). He calls our bluff. He knows that we know that He knows our hearts.

Secretly, we know that if we ever do get involved —seriously and sincerely—with our Maker, we will never be able to come up with a legitimate reason to back down and out. Intellectually, we know that God has us pegged perfectly. It's not the wrongness of the Bible that bothers us; it's its rightness. Right?

[1]Dr. Dale Lockhart, "Everything's Up to Date in Kansas City," *Good News,* (United Methodist Church Publication), July-September, 1970.
[2]Dr. Richard Barbour, "You and Y," San Diego, *Evening Tribune,* October 31, 1970.
[3]RNS, "Nudity in Church Called 'Respectful'," *Milwaukee Journal,* June 13, 1970.

9

"People no longer have religion."

"We are at a loss to say where we are religiously. We do not know what we believe. The outlines of traditional conviction have been softened, and we prefer to float in this blurred climate."[1]

Six percent of Denverites are now primarily concerned about the fate of religion.

What has become of America, the *Christian* Nation?

During the first week of November, 1970, we asked our radio audience to phone in to our daily talk program, Counsel and Comment, and tell us why they thought the church attendance and giving were generally on the decline.

Their comments were interesting. The liberal churches were accused of being dead and preaching a dead God—of having no relevancy or spiritual food.

The conservatives needed a revival from spiritual sleep. They were lethargic and cold—not the least bit excited about Christ.

Pastors, all too often, "knew it all" and were too dogmatic and legalistic. "There seems to be more emphasis on organization than on people, on increasing numbers than on helping people."

Too frequently, newcomers find it difficult to break the barriers of exclusive clubs and cliques of some fundamental churches. The goal seems to be: Let's see how many people we can keep out. You have no hope of ever being accepted unless you get the knack of hairsplitting the group way, right or wrong. Instead of The Church being a spiritual melting-pot, it has become a kettle of contention.

While the pulpit and the pew are not innocent, the stay-at-home delinquents are not without guilt. Many said they were too lazy to attend church or lacked interest. Some didn't want to be reminded that they were not living right. In addition, some of the "pillars" have been supporting nature on the weekend instead of the church.

". . . some church members are settling for do-it-yourself-worship. They claim to be worshipping God at the beach, in the mountains, or in front of their TV screen. One minister tried to cope with the problem by suggesting a do-it-yourself worship kit for his do-it-yourself worshippers. He recommended a portable pew; an abridged songbook; an abbreviated New Testament; a mouth organ to substitute for the church organ; a set of responsive readings, suitable for use wherever there is an echo; a miniature offering plate. 'The size of the plate doesn't matter,' the minister argued, 'since the worshipper will get his offering back anyway.' The minister also gave the additional advice that the service would be enhanced if, at its conclusion, the worshipper would rush to a mirror somewhere and shake hands with himself."[2]

Politics is another reason for the decline of the church's effectiveness. Colorado Governor, John A. Love, addressing the Board Meeting of the Homeland Ministries of the United Church of Christ, in Denver, January, 1971, said: "If the church takes to the streets, we shall have lost a posture and stature which can serve us well in the trying times ahead.

"Churches," he warned, "can lose their effectiveness by involving themselves in political issues." He asked church leaders and pastors to stick to matters of the spirit and let the experts handle the issues of politics, war and the like.[3]

Dr. Dean Rusk, for eight years U. S. Secretary of State, now teaching at the University of Georgia, was asked by two editors to comment on the church's involvement in the peace movement.

"I think it is appropriate for the churches to consider these issues and to speak out on them," he responded, "and churches have no obligation, as such, to support the government of the U. S., nor to take any particular view that might come from the political process of the country."

The former Secretary of State stressed, however, that churches should speak on their own commitments. "What I am interested in is whether the churches are, in fact, all of them, really basing their views on their own commitments to peace in the world."

He expressed doubt that many "peace groups" are genuinely interested in peace since they criticize the United States for involvement in Vietnam and never "call upon Hanoi, Peking and North Korea to stop what they are doing."[4]

The hippie movement believes Americans have badly bungled the affluence test, and a seminary president feels that the church definitely mishandled prosperity when it came fifteen years ago. Both the clergy and the laity let the culture—rather than the spirit of Christ—dictate the uses of prosperity.

Consequently, the Christians' life style moved up with the income. Very few maintained the modest "pilgrim and stranger" outlook. Pastors welcomed the better way of life. Few of them taught the flock that the God-given prosperity was for the Gospel's promotion and not for their own.

As a further result, prosperity and the "instant" era sharpened our materialistic appetites while deadening our spiritual senses. "Living in heavenly places with Christ" became a neglected and distant truth to the credit card-carrying Christian.

Editor Arthur J. Moore, Jr. said that "getting and spending is what our society is all about and a little divine sanction will speed up the process.

"But," he continued, "idolatry by definition is the substitution of the lesser for the greater. This is what the young and the idealistic in our society (and in Soviet society and in the majority of societies on the earth today) are trying to tell us . . .

"We are all in chains of our own making. The Incarnation sets us free not to self-congratulation but to the realization that we are in chains. We are free to free ourselves, but not ourselves alone. For we must free our brothers to free ourselves.'"⁵

Then there is the subject of a cut-rate clergy that, while supposedly representing God and Company, has its hand out for the no-less-than 10 percent discount from the embarrassed businessman. But lest the layman see "love of money" only in the shepherds of the soul, let him ask how much money he'd give to the church if none of it were tax deductible?

Religion is in trouble in America today because of misrepresentation. We have been pushing an egocentric rather than a self-denying philosophy. We have been asking: What's in it for me? rather than, what does God require of me?

True religion is not a utility. God will not be manipulated. He is no cosmic bellhop that does our bidding. If we start out with the intention of using God for our personal advantage, there is no hope of our developing a close relationship with Him. We will experience no benefits nor will we encounter God in a satisfying way. Is it any wonder, then, that so few Americans have an interest in God?

"A mistaken view of prayer (that God is a wish-granter), implanted or encouraged by parents, may cause a youngster to become an atheist in his teens.

"He views God relationship exactly backwards. Instead of seeing himself as the creature and servant of God, a child sees himself as the center of the universe, and sees God as a genie whose role is to protect and please him—children should be taught from the very start to pray in the Spirit of Jesus."⁶

This is not to say that our relationship with God is one-sided. He does daily load us with benefits; He is a present help in time of need; the Lord is my shepherd, I shall not want. We can never outdo or outgive God, but all these things are a result of the right kind of relationship between God and one who worships Him. I believe our primary concern should not be how God can help us but how we can glorify Him.

Even in Christ-centered churches, all too often the pastor is trying to "evangelize the world" instead of training workers.

"SHEEP HAVE SHEEP: Winning souls is the presenting of Jesus, who is the Christ, to unsaved men wherever they are, whenever we have the chance, and seeing the miracle of repentance and the birth of a new creature. This task is to be done by the pulpit and the pew. The pulpit is to train the pew to do it. Some laymen have thought that when no one accepted Christ, it was a sign that the pastor was losing his power. Don't you know that shepherds do not have sheep? Sheep have sheep. Every saved soul is saved to help save others. The Sunday morning worship service too often does not confront sinners with Christ. You know as well as I do that sinners are not coming to church. They are where the Bible said they would be, in the highways and hedges (Edward V. Hill)."[7]

If we are speaking of the man-made religions of the world, then I will be the first to agree with you that—generally—religions are of little value, but if we are talking about an encounter with the one and only Living God, then we are talking about the greatest thing in the world.

Writing to Timothy, Apostle Paul says this about God: "Who will have all men to be saved, and to come unto the knowledge of the truth" (1 Tim. 2:4).

To be valuable, religion must do two fundamental things. First, it must give us the knowledge of the truth or true knowledge. Not only must it give us the truth about science and history; but what is more important, it must give us the truth about ourselves.

No religion should be exempt from the test of truth. Every religion should be prepared to face facts and give facts. If science produces facts, how much more should religion? If a court case demands the truth, the whole truth and nothing but the truth, how much more should religion be truthful? If a doctor's prescription requires accurate facts, how much more should be required from a religion? If the building of a bridge necessitates precise specifications and figures, what shall we say about the meaning of life? If we find it so important to be properly informed about space travel, isn't it more important to be knowledgeable about this life and the life hereafter?

The greatest obstacle to the discovery of Living Truth is religion without proven facts. A truthless religion closes the mind to truth. The superficial, legalistic knowledge of the Pharisees and Sadducees was what caused them to reject Truth when they saw Him.

In addition to truthfulness, a religion must be able to save. Notice that Apostle Paul said that all must "come to the knowledge of truth" *and* "be saved." God's truth not only informs but it saves. Divine truth is living and energizing; it makes men out of us. It gives us character and integrity. It makes us honest. It pumps moral convictions into our bloodstream. It gives us the desire to quit lying, cheating and stealing.

Our religion should be able to give us courage in danger, comfort in sorrow, and faith in the face of formidable obstacles. It should be able to dispel fear and destroy hatred. It should develop compassion and give a solid hope for the future.

Philosophy permits only the possibility of a life after death, but it is Christianity's unique message that proclaims positively and unequivocally that "This mortal shall put on immortality!" Christ lives again and so shall we.

Why do I like Christianity? There are many good reasons. I like the Christian message because it saves "to the uttermost (all) that come unto God" by Jesus Christ. I like the message of Christianity because it is a message of concern for the individual. It is a true map to "life more abundant." It clearly shows me my present location, where I need to go and how I can get there.

I like the message of Jesus Christ because it fully meets my needs. It clothes the naked; it feeds the hungry. It provides forgiveness for sin and freedom from its guilt. It is no respecter of persons. It provides a place for the thief, the harlot and the murderer. It would have us all to be saved and come to know the Lord Jesus Christ.

If ever America needed to know these truths, it is now. "True religion and undefiled" would not only be concerned about the problems of increased crime and corrupt government, but it would make changes for the better because of changed and better citizens.

"You ask me what is the greatest menace and enemy to our boys and girls and our homes, and I will not tell you it is the movie, the dance, booze, or the gambling den. I will tell you it is the scarcity of Christian mothers and Christian fathers.

"Give us more Christian homes and we will do away with drunkards, gamblers, and theives; for the normal way to do away with such is to quit producing them.

"The crime problem can't be solved by more police, more radio-equipped squad cars and more jails. Nor will it be solved by more high-salaried descendants of monkeys teaching their pernicious doctrine of evolution in the colleges and universities of the land. Nor will it be solved by more bellowing, modernistic, Christ-dishonoring preachers, who have taken the depravity out of man, the deity out of Christ, the blood out of the atonement, the inspiration out of the Bible, the fire out of hell and the power out of conversion. The remedy lies in more old-fashioned home example and home religion, more homes where family prayers are offered. There is not another influence to be found on earth that is equal to the family altar. Family prayer builds walls of protection around the home and the children. God pity the child that comes into the home where none prays."[8]

Originally, the Republic of the United States of America was intentionally and specifically established to be a unique nation under God. The constitution and the principles on which it stands were reverently and humbly founded on the Sacred Scriptures. Now, when America shuts the doors of its educational institutions to God and His Word, she is divorcing herself from Him Who made her great.

Is it true that we no longer need God? Are we able to get along without Him? Can affluence and technology take the place of God? You have only to read the front page of today's newspaper to realize that we are still very much in need of Almighty God. Will we be too hardheaded, too proud to confess our backsliding, to admit our waywardness and helplessness; or will we humble ourselves before our God so that He can heal our land?

We will never return to the old America; we are too old and weak to go back, and youth is not interested. We can only grow and develop, though painfully at times.

But there has to be an immovable point of reference to provide stability and meaning. There is really only one area to which we can and should return, and that is to basic Bible beliefs.

Some things are never old-fashioned or outdated: faith, hope and love. Who protests the sun's rising and setting on schedule? On the contrary, we expect it. It is reassuring that the tide comes in and goes out regularly. Bible ethics, virtues and truth are also timeless and changeless, and for this we should be grateful. What is already complete and perfect has no need of improvement or adjustment.

Some of us still believe that God is only in *our* camp and in our interpretations of the Bible. But everyone cannot be right. It is better to lose face and change than hold out stubbornly to the end—the wrong end. The time is long overdue when laymen, pastors and church leaders stop operating on a denominational level and begin living on the Divine level.

Let us concentrate on what unites us—Christ—and minimize what divides us—distinctive interpretations. Have we forgotten that we need each other —that we are members of one body?

In eternity, it will matter little whether or not we recruited members to our particular camp. What about the ones who rejected the entire Gospel because they were offended by our doctrinal divisions?

At times, one wonders if we are the defenders of the faith or of the fate of our theological sand castles. Obviously, we are not defending the same faith, only our own idea of "the faith."

If God is really getting all the glory and the credit, why are we so protective, so much on the defensive? Whose reputation is at stake: God's or ours?

What has become of "in honor preferring one another?" What's happened to "he that is greatest among you . . . be your servant?"

Whenever we see some independent soul "casting out devils," Jesus chides us: "Forbid him not; for he that is not against us is for us" (Luke 9:50).

Do you hear the prophet Jeremiah saying, "This is a nation that obeyeth not the voice of the Lord their God, nor receiveth correction; truth is perished, and is cut off from their mouth" (Jeremiah 7:28)? Through the lips of the same prophet, God warns, "that nation will I punish; that nation I will destroy." It is bad enough for a nation to forsake God, but woe to the nation that is forsaken by God.

The way back is still open. Although Revelation 2:5 is a message primarily to the church, its principle applies to nations that once knew God: "Remember therefore from whence thou art fallen, and repent, and do the first works; or else I will come unto thee quickly, and will remove thy candlestick out of his place, except thou repent."

A nation repents as its people repent, and the masses repent as its leaders repent. Nineveh repented and was spared God's wrath but only because they took God's warning seriously and repented, "from the greatest of them even to the least of them." There is little hope of salvation from the judgment of God upon America unless there is a thorough turning to God on the part of our President, our state representatives, our administrators, professors, and our "men of God"—the pastors and preachers of our land.

Many people do not attend church because they say that "you can't find God in church anymore." This was the title of an article in the March 1969 issue of *Ladies Home Journal*. It seems that in many churches you can hear something about everything except about God and how to know Him.

Our survey showed that the thing that bothered people the most was the feeling that many of the worshippers were hypocrites. Only 3 percent said they attended church because they liked to hear the priest or pastor preach. 9 percent liked the music more than they did the sermon. Only 8 percent felt that the sermon was the high point of the service.

The survey showed that people want more from the pulpit than pious platitudes or views and opinions on social or political trends. They want to know how to apply Christianity to everyday living.

It goes without saying that if we want to turn the tide against crime, violence, permissiveness, sex perversion, drugs and pornography, we are going to have to turn back to God and back to the Bible.

No time for God? No time to read His Word and to serve Him? No time for laying up treasures in Heaven rather than on earth?

God is able to give plenty of time. All it takes is a great depression, or a revolution or an enemy attack! All we need is coast-to-coast sabotage of our public transportation and utilities. Any one or all of these "divine paddles" are capable of bringing spiritual matters into proper perspective.

"BLACK MOUNTAIN, N. C. (RNS)—Evangelist Billy Graham told the International Students Association at Montreat-Anderson College that 'it is an illusion that freedom can survive without religious faith.'

"Holding that the U.S., if it does not change its course, is heading for a dictatorship, he said, 'I don't know if it's to the right or left . . . but in our search for new freedom, we are in danger of losing what little freedom we have.'

"Mr. Graham said an 'anarchic' attitude is growing, an 'attitude that wants to tear down everything and put nothing in its place. The only thing that can turn the tide,' he added, 'is a religious revival.'

"In one sense, we're all brothers and sisters around the world, but in a spiritual sense, we are not,' the evangelist said."[9]

To bring God's inevitable judgment upon herself, America needs only to continue on her present course. I believe that America, currently, is on a collision course with the judgment of God. There is but one way to avert God's just punishment on our nation and that is to act on 2 Chronicles 7:14. "If my people, which are called by my name, shall humble themselves and pray, and seek my face, and turn from their wicked ways; then will I hear from heaven, and will forgive their sin, and will heal their land."

Today, let us walk humbly before the Lord and pray for our community, for our country, for men in high places—that God would have mercy on us and send a nationwide spiritual awakening. Let each individual accept this concern personally and pray and work to that end.

[1]Samuel H. Miller, *Religion in a Technical Age,* (Harvard University Press, Cambridge, Mass. 1968), p. 9.

[2]Published by Haven of Rest, Hollywood, California, 90028. Bob Bowman, *The Log of the Good Ship Grace* (Vol. 37, No. 3, 1971), p. 11.

[3]"Newscope" *United Church Herald,* January 1971, p. 28.

[4]"Rusk on Church Peace Pronouncements," *Religious News Service,* December 7, 1970.

[5]*Religious News Service,* December 10, 1970.

[6]Louis Cassel's, "Wrong Prayer View Can Foster Atheism," *The Denver Post,* November 14, 1970, p. 6.

[7]*Decision Magazine,* March 1971, p. 14.

[8]Rev. Lincicome, *Enemies of the Home* (Drayton, N. Dakota; Square Deal Printing Co., 1934), p. 31.

[9]Religious News Service.

10

"We have toothless law enforcement."

"Lawlessness shall greatly increase."—Jesus Christ

The cancer of crime has been multiplying at an alarming rate. Serious crimes went up 148 percent between 1960 and 1969. During the same period our population increased 13 percent. "Crime in the '60s increased 11 times as fast as the population."[1]

In the meantime, *concern* about crime drastically decreased. Only 3 percent of those interviewed were primarily concerned about lawlessness. Immediately, we are faced with two disturbing trends: crime increase, concern decrease.

Can we hope for a reversal? I believe that will depend on what we add to our hope. I think that the main clue to the resolution of the crime problem can be found in the attitude of the 97 percent who are not sufficiently concerned with law enforcement.

The Judiciary

For years the courts of our land have been under attack for a variety of abuses and for inefficiency: 1) not enough time on the bench; 2) leniency; 3) decisions based on a whim, on the time of day, on weather conditions; 4) involvement in pre-trial bargaining; 5) refusing to see or admit evidence; 6) political and criminal pressures and connection; 7) reversing convictions on a technicality; 8) pulling rank.

All of these accusations, and others, have been sufficiently substantiated, but it would certainly be unjust to imply that these deficiencies are rampant. Honorable jurists do not justify these deplorable situations, and they would appreciate a realistic viewpoint on the part of the public. What the judiciary needs is more understanding, fairness, practical help and general support. They are representing the citizens of the land. We need to pull together, not apart.

Our courts are struggling to operate under an unbelievable burden of diverse handicaps. Using horse and buggy procedures, they are trying to move in a technological space age. The number of judges has not kept up with the population explosion.

Simultaneously, the courts are endeavoring to catch up on a backlog of pending cases and to modernize an archaic judiciary system—"But this is the way it has always been done." It is a long, complicated and almost impossible process. Standardization of procedures and penalties is desperately needed but is sabotaged by jurisdictional wrangling.

The Police

The jurists rightly expect the police not to break any laws that regulate them while they are enforcing laws for others. The police department is expected to abide by the constitution and by legislated rules and regulations. He who is specifically assigned to enforce the laws of the land—be it a police officer, an attorney or a judge—should be the first to obey those laws and in this way influence others by good example.

Even the atheists in the Soviet Union, after many years of trial and error, have finally come up with what has been Jesus' teaching all along: courtesy brings better results than does rudeness. It frequently happens that good police work—solving a difficult case—goes by with no special thanks from the public. But a small, common courtesy on the part of an officer draws out a public acknowledgement from some grateful citizen.

The public would like to see the judiciary and the police department improve their relationship. They are *not* in competition with each other. Their ultimate objectives are identical.

It is imperative that there be realistic cooperation and coordination between police and court work, because while the courts are having to postpone trials, the criminals are not calling a time out. Then too, probation is only as good as the lawbreaker's will to go straight. The best probation officer in the world is helpless where there is no desire to change.

As a pastor, may I also remind our law and justice departments that even the U. S. Supreme Court is not "Supreme." There is a higher court, presided by The Chief Justice of the Universe. Before Him we will all stand, stripped of our titles and vestures. We will all be just plain, ordinary citizens of the world, before Him who is "no respecter of persons." To Him we will give a full account of all the "deeds done in the body, whether they be good or bad," and we will "tell the truth, the whole truth, and nothing but the truth." The judgment will be just. All the wrongs will be made right. Justice shall triumph at last.

For the time being, we all have been given a suspended sentence. Each one of us is on probation and in his own custody. The Divine Supreme Court has even provided a Probation Officer—should we be interested in His help and services. His guidance and strength are available to all. He is the Third Person of the Trinity—the Holy Spirit. He is able to retrain us to the extent that not only we ourselves will be pleased, but even The Chief Justice will say, "Well done!"

The Public

Law enforcement is not simply a matter of good police work; it involves the entire community: children, parents, teachers, preachers, policemen, attorneys, jurists and community leaders. There can be no successful crime control without the cooperation of every citizen. It is a matter of simple arithmetic, if nothing else.

Can we hope for the support of the average "law-abiding citizen?" Hardly. ". . . business and property crimes, ranging from embezzlement to shoplifting and vandalism, are draining off . . . 13 billion dollars from the nation's economy."[2] Keep in mind that this is not organized crime. Most of this is not the work of the poor, underprivileged, uneducated minority. This is the affluent, "respectable" and sophisticated majority.

You can understand why I am not as concerned about the street and syndicated crime as I am with that which is being committed by the "upright" citizen. We are paying an additional 15 percent for every item we buy because manufacturers, wholesalers and retailers add this amount in order to cover employee thefts.

We are talking about respected citizens and community leaders. "One example: In a New York suburban store, 29 part-time employees were involved in theft. Most held two jobs so they could afford to live in the community—and the store, furthermore, carried items they needed in their new homes.

"Twenty-one had college degrees. Four were attending college. Two were elementary-school principals and one was a parochial-school principal."[3]

Our problem does not lie in organized crime. Syndicated crime—the underworld—exists only because we—the citizens—allow it to exist. Organized crime is a parasite; it needs something on which to feed. *America* is supporting corruption to the tune of $19.7 billion a year. I believe we have this "underground" corruption only because of the corruption above the ground.

Tragically, many a contemporary American is trained to ignore or break the law from the minute he is born. It used to be that a crime was a crime—period. Later, it was wrong only if you were caught. Now, even if you're caught, arrested, tried and indicted, you are not necessarily a convicted criminal.

Respect for law and order begins in the home. Parents can encourage their children to watch television programs that put the police and the courtroom in a good light. It would help if children understand more about the difficult task of law enforcement and crime fighting. School children would benefit much from seeing courtroom action first-hand. Let us remember that children learn best by example. The public school and the church school teachers are also a powerful source of influence on the attitude of the child toward the law.

The people who complain about the sad situation of crime and punishment are often the least involved in community affairs. Law enforcement is everyone's full-time responsibility; it is everybody's moral obligation. The fight against crime can never be just a job or a way of making a living. Crime affects the entire community. But how can we prosecute the criminal if some refuse to press charges? Some are more concerned about the money they will lose on the job than that a thief is turned loose to steal again and again. Is this not being an accessory before and after the fact? I believe it is.

A good place to begin supporting *our* police, *our* attorneys and *our* jurists is to send them that long-overdue note of appreciation for the "thankless" job they are doing. Certainly they get paid for what they are doing, but so does the postman, the paper boy and the delivery man, the service station attendant, the shop clerk and the bank teller.

When was the last time—or even the first time—we took the time to thank the local policeman for serving our community? Believe it or not, he's human too. When did we call the chief of police, not to make a complaint, but simply to tell him thanks for fighting crime? And did we ever get in touch with an attorney or a judge to encourage them?

It's a place to start—a place to start the hard pull toward the moral principles that once made this country great and the envy of nations. Maybe we will even rediscover the Ten Commandments and the Golden Rule. Remember the days when we treated them right and they were good to us?

[1]"Crime Expense Now Up to 51 Billion a Year," *U. S. News & World Report,* October 26, 1970, page 31.
[2]Op cit., "Crime Expense . . .", p. 30.
[3]Ibid.

11

"I don't think it will ever be any better."

"I have a wonderful confidence in the American people. They have met many challenges along the way and come out on top." This was one respondent's reply to the survey question: In the next five to ten years, do you think America will be better off or worse off than it is today?

In spite of this one individual's bright outlook, Americans generally are not so optimistic about the future. Fewer than half of the respondents are confident that America will be better off than it is today in the next five to ten years, *but* almost two out of three anticipate their personal status will improve in the same time period.

Nationally, some of the "optimists" felt that things would become better because "things can't get much worse."

Many measured improvement and success in dollars and cents.

"We've got many things paid for and don't intend to take on any more debts, so it stands to reason we'll be better off."

"I won't be working by then, so I'll be worse off."

"Inflation will be twice as bad."

"I don't think it will ever be any better with the government wasting all the taxpayer's money."

Some felt that the end of their world had come because they lost their job or had their car repossessed.

But not everybody related a good or bad future to money.

"I look for bigger and better things because I feel a person who will work for a goal will make it eventually."

"I have a pretty nice family. As the years go by they get better and better."

Of those interviewed, no one mentioned the possibility of a third world war. Do we have any reason to expect war with the Soviet Union. How much substance is there to the alleged Communist conspiracy to overthrow our present system of government? Who wants to know? Who cares?

Invaders usually do not announce their intentions in advance. Gerald Clarke, in a *"Time* Essay," reminds us of the ways of history. "World War III? One can only hope—and add unhappily that few people in January 1914 predicted World War I."[1]

I doubt that the majority of Americans is concerned about either the fact or the fiction of an impending nuclear war or of a sinister plot to take over our country by more-or-less peaceful means. I believe the average American man is more interested in the scoreboard than he is in how many Soviet agents are operating in our fifty States.

Even when it's staring you in the face, you don't want to believe what you see. You don't like what you see, and you wish you hadn't seen it. You try to forget it. You hope it will go away while you're ignoring it. But rather than go away, it only continues to gain strength.

"Humanity in a crisis is generally insensitive to the gravity of the times in which it lives. Men do not want to believe their own times are wicked, partly because it involves too much self-accusation and principally because they have no standard outside of themselves by which to measure their times. If there is no fixed concept of justice, how shall men know it is violated?"[2]

Since our enemy has us sized up rather well, I feel it would be only fair play to understand them a little better. What is international Communism's basic philosophy and objective? *They are sworn to world domination.* "There exists a world Communist movement, a worldwide revolutionary movement whose purpose it is to establish a Communist totalitarian dictatorship in the countries throughout the world."[3]

How does this affect the United States? "The Communist leaders say that the transition from the imperfect society of Socialism to the perfect society of Communism cannot take place until the Free World (the United States and its allies) is defeated. The overthrow of Capitalism, then, is the prerequisite for the establishment of Communism. The Communist must use any device to accomplish this end. Infiltration of every major phase of a free society must take place: government, labor, communications, entertainment, art, literature, education and even religious institutions. Of great importance is the fact that they seek ópinion-molding positions in all spheres of society."[4]

From the start, the Communists have been using an advanced type of weapon. ". . . psychological warfare . . . the corruption of human reason, the dimming of the human intellect and the disintegration of the moral and spiritual life of one nation by the influence of the will of another . . ."[5]

It is estimated by the experts that the United

States lags up to 40 years behind the Communists in political warfare. ". . . Czechoslovakia fell into the Soviet orbit . . . an entire nation was captured (1948) from within, without a single soldier firing as much as a single shot. A badly frightened world realized that warfare had now entered into a new dimension. A large measure of our long list of defeats and reverses, vis-a-vis the Communists, since the end of World War II, can be attributed to the inability of western leadership to grasp and cope with this new problem."[6]

The Communists have had time to become experts in this field. "Perhaps the most important point of all, it is essential to attack the enemy nation in its weak spot (and what nation has not its weak spot?) to undermine, crush, break down its resistance, and convince it that it is being deceived, misled and brought to destruction by its own government, in order that it may lose confidence in the justice of its cause and thus the opposition at home (and what nation is without one?) may raise its head and make trouble more successfully than before. The original well-knit, solid, powerful fabric of the enemy nation must be gradually disintegrated, broken down, rotted, so that it falls to pieces like a fungus when one treads upon it in a forest."[7]

Former U. S. Ambassador to Russia and France, William Bullitt says that Communists are essentially super-criminals who have their own set of laws or lack of them. The average westerner finds it impossible to comprehend a Communist's total depravity and cynicism. "The great tragedy of the West is that its leaders—and they are all good, Christian patriotic men—simply are incapable of grasping or understanding the nature of the enemy bent upon their destruction."[8]

If the Communist conspiracy is an actuality, why don't our presidents or vice-presidents talk about it? The record shows that potential presidents and vice-presidents who speak out on the subject never make it to the top.

"With Marxism taking the world, our leaders don't even mention the Communist menace but talk of 'building bridges of friendship.' No candidate for the presidency or vice-presidency—except George Wallace and Ronald Reagan—even mention the Communist scourge. They play like it doesn't exist."[9]

So who cares if "America (is) a land in which workers get paid for not working, preachers get paid for not believing, teachers get paid for anarchy, mothers get paid for not marrying, farmers get paid for not farming, and promoters get paid for fertilizer tanks which ain't?"[10]

Not very efficient, you say? Bound to ruin us, you think? We are right on schedule. Karl Marx' dying words were: "Spend them to death." We won't let him down.

To hear the Social Gospellers tell it, you'd think Jesus was a socialistic idealist and a Communist in good standing. They insist that He was an anti-capitalist and that He came to solve all of our social ills. Nothing of the kind! "Jesus didn't take the people out of the slums; he took the slums out of the people. Jesus did not minister to groups; he ministered to individuals."[11]

I cannot think of a more anti-materialistic incident in the life of Jesus than the one in Luke 12:13-15 (LNT): "Then someone called from the crowd, 'Sir,

109

please tell my brother to divide my father's estate with me.' But Jesus replied, 'Man, who made Me a judge over you to decide such things as that? Beware! Don't always be wishing for what you don't have.' "

Let me say at this point that I am disturbed by our war-protesting clergy. Very few Americans actually want war, but let us be careful not to destroy patriotism while we are combating war. I am not for war for the sake of war. I know I am not an imperialistic warmonger. But while I am for peace, I am not for peace at any price.

I wish I could say that we should not be too hard on our war-protesting clergy. I wish I could encourage everyone to allow them to protest against our government to their hearts content while they still can, because when the "others" take over, this inalienable right of free speech will no longer exist. (You know what happens to protesting preachers in the Soviet Union.)

But conspiracy is hard to see or touch. Let's forget about the fifth column and pretend it doesn't exist. Let's talk about the things we can see and touch— like a U.S.S.R. nuclear submarine, carrying 16 nuclear naval missiles, each one with a potential range of more than 5,000 miles. What about the Soviet subs and ships sailing the seven seas? How many are there and what are they for? "Russian fleet activity in the open seas is today five times greater than it was four years ago.

"The Russians maintain some 1500 naval vessels in commission; in the next fiscal year the active operational fleet of the United States may drop to about 550 vessels.

"The Russian submarine fleet is still in many ways the most important element of the Soviet Navy, not only because of its great size (395 submarines, as against Germany's 57 when World War II started) but also because of the new role of the nuclear-powered submarine as a missile platform, with the capability of landing a knockout punch against any land target on earth."[12]

"Russia's intercontinental-range strike forces already have six times as much nuclear explosive power as the U.S. and at the present growth rate, the ratio in 1975 will be 12 or 15 to 1.

"At present, the U.S. is reducing its overseas commitments, cutting back on its armed forces and maintaining a numerical ceiling on its missile arsenal, while the Soviets pursue an exactly opposite course.

"In the . . . mathematics of nuclear weaponing, this gives the Russians an arsenal, measured in destructive megatons, six times as large as that of the U.S.

"Weakness on the part of the United States is an invitation to disaster.

"Right now, judging from their results, the Soviets are putting the equivalent of about three billion dollars more a year into defense-related technology than we are."[13]

". . . the Russians are building eight Polaris type submarines a year and about six other nuclear-powered submarines, while the United States is standing still."[14]

I will not bore you with more facts and figures (although there is much more where this came from), but let me ask you a question. Why this build-up when the Soviet Government knows that we are cutting back both in arms and in men? Do you honestly believe the Communists will let us live the way we want to? Peace they want, and they want it desperately—but they insist on their own brand.

Do we doubt that they would start dropping atomic bombs simply because we would reciprocate? Do you think they consider human life sacred? No, it is the *cause* that counts. Never would they hesitate to trigger a nuclear war, even though they would lose some of their own people. They only need to be convinced they will win. ". . . there is nothing in Soviet military literature, published for the guidance of commanders, on the subject of 'overkill.' On the contrary, Russian theoreticians emphasize the 'one-act war' with stress on the surprise use of overwhelming force."[15]

The Soviets know that we are basically a peace-loving nation. They know that we are merciful and bighearted. We alleviate hunger; they are known to have produced famines intentionally.

The Communists would strike the U.S. if America refuses to be intimidated.

"The U.S.S.R. is clearly striving to achieve a first-strike capability, which could be used to blackmail the United States.

". . . the United States is far more vulnerable to annihilation in a surprise attack than the Soviet Union because of the latter's larger land areas.

"The planners are inclined to think the percentage may be even higher by 1975, given a nominal improvement in Soviet missile accuracy and the fact that Russia may be able to assign two warheads to each U.S. missile site—and still have 500 left over to send against cities.

"The Russians' announcements that they have repeatedly fired missiles over 8,000 miles and hit less than 1½ miles off target are not dismissed by the Pentagon experts.

"One of the Navy's admirals argues that the existing concentration of land-based missiles, population and industry is an invitation to annihilation by Russia."[16]

There is a difference between fatalism and realism. While I do not expect real and lasting peace until Christ's return, I do not feel we should just watch things happen.

"Nowhere in the Holy Writings is there any premise for the modern belief that universal peace will be achieved by the works of man or the plans of human leaders. Jesus warned His followers of the folly of such false hopes, and told us in plain words that wars would continue intermittently until the end of the Gospel age.

"The Book of Revelation portrays a warring world at the very minute Christ returns, and definitely states that there can be no peace until He who is Prince of Peace, returns to establish His Kingdom."[17]

Regardless of what happens, the future is bright for the child of God, for he shall reign with the Prince of Peace in His eternal kingdom. But I cannot believe that Americans would capitulate to International Communism. I believe we would rather be "dead than red." (If rumors are right, the Communists, in the event of a take-over, do not intend for those of us who are over thirty to be even "red." Since they don't believe they will be able to re-educate us, they will simply "eliminate" us.)

I have not shared this threat of nuclear annihilation to stir up an anti-communistic spirit. Only when we become anti-sin will God's judgment be averted. God will bless America—if America will bless God.

[1]*Time,* February 15, 1971.

[2]Bishop Fulton Sheen, *Communism and the Conscience of the West,* Bobbs-Merrill, 1948.

[3]From the Internal Security Act, passed by Congress, 1950.

[4]*A Manual for Survival,* Compiled and Published by The Church League of America, Wheaton, Illinois, 1961, p. 12.

[5]Op cit., *Manual for Survival,* p. 21.

[6]Op Cit., *Manual for Survival,* p. 22.

[7]Op cit., *Manual for Survival,* p. 21. (Quoting Ewald Banse, a pre-Hitler military psychologist in Germany, 1932).

[8]Op cit., *Manual for Survival,* p. 40.

[9]Tom Anderson, Editor, Farm & Ranch Magazine, *Vital Speeches,* May 15, 1970, p. 462.

[10]Op cit., *Vital Speeches,* p. 462.

[11]Op cit., *Vital Speeches,* p. 460.

[12]Hanson W. Baldwin, "Russia's Big Red Fleet," *Readers' Digest,* November, 1970, p. 195.

[13]"Russia vs. U. S.—Coming Crisis In Arms," *U.S. News and World Report,* November 30, 1970, p. 24.

[14]"Russians Really Coming" says Admiral, *Rocky Mountain News,* Denver, February 23, 1971, p. 24.

[15]"Is U.S. Forfeiting the Arms Race to Russia?" *U. S. News & World Report,* October 19, 1970, p. 24.

[16]Ibid, p. 24.

[17]Harry Rimmer, *The Coming War and the Rise of Russia,* Wm. B. Eerdman's Publishing Co., Grand Rapids, Michigan, 1944, pp. 15, 84.

12

"We all figure in God's problems."

Does anyone care to listen to God's number one problem? Is there anyone who would be interested in God's solution of His one problem?

God does have a real problem and only one. He also has a solution—only one—but it is a good one. It works every time and has a perfect record.

Fortunately, we all figure in God's problem. In fact, we are all deeply involved in His problem. The only thing needed is for us to become sufficiently concerned about this situation. How we react to God's dilemma will have a drastic and immediate effect on the resolution of our own problems. And if God's primary problem does not become our primary concern, we can expect little, if any, improvement or change in regard to our own current concerns.

God is not saying that our problems do not exist or that they are not important. He is saying that His problem is more important. In fact, it supersedes all other problems. He is saying that our concerns are superficial by comparison. He wants us to realize something else—that all of our problems are the direct result of His problem.

We do have an ecological problem, but it is the result of the pollution of our hearts and minds.

Crime is a concern, but how concerned are we about breaking the laws of God?

Religion is important, but not if it does not involve doing God's will.

Morality is a problem, but it will become more of a problem if we all end up doing that which is right in our own eyes and pretend that divine absolutes don't exist.

Finances are a problem, but only because we really serve Mammon rather than God.

Peace on earth is an impossibility, unless earthlings make their peace with Heaven.

Drugs are an escape from reality, but self-deception is just as effective. Drugs blow your mind and leave it damaged. God, on the contrary, expands the mind to new dimensions and heals it in the process.

Certainly we have reason to be concerned about government, but how are we allowing God to govern our private lives?

We do have a public relations problem, but first we need to come into a right relationship with God. Name any existing personal or social problem, and the Bible will trace its source to a breakdown in our relationship with our Creator.

God's number one problem is sin. God's number one concern is mankind. And God's number one solution is Jesus. This interesting development goes back before time began.

God foresaw the problem. After eliminating all the ideas that wouldn't work, the Trinity programmed a plan that would work. No need now for trial and error on our part; no need for alternate solutions. God ran every possibility through the celestial computers to test its feasibility. Only one system met the requirements.

God masterminded a completely unexpected plan

called "Christ Crucified." In the plan were incorporated features that would automatically trigger specific reactions from the pseudo-righteous and the proud. Today, most people know that the plan does strike many as being foolish, and others find it offensive. But, on the positive side, the plan does everything it was programmed to do. One needs only to experiment with the plan to discover that it actually has full redemptive capability. It does what no other plan can do.

The way of good works doesn't work because it would disqualify most of us on earth and the rest of us in heaven. God says that even our best efforts are soiled by hypocrisy and pride. We can never balance our vices by our virtues because, in God's pure eyes, even our virtues are defective.

But even if we could become truly good as of now, what about our past sins and guilt? We should be only grateful for His preparing a program that would take care of the past, the present and the future. God anticipated every problem and every complication. He came up with a workable solution to every problem.

When we cooperate with Him, God not only forgives all of our sins forever, He also gives us the necessary ability to forgive ourselves. In addition to this, He gives us the capability to resist further temptation and to live a life that is pleasing to Him.

I would do well to believe God's analysis and diagnosis of man's ills. I would be wise to accept His prescription and to take His medicine. I can put full confidence in His ability because it was He who put me together, and I can trust His motives because He proved His love to me when He took my punishment. Christ died for me, and His mission was successful because God raised Him from the dead.

I may not understand it all, but I can experience it all. How? Simply, and again I say, simply by believing the story and having believed it, by receiving Christ into my being. Why is this so necessary? Because the Spirit of Christ, living in me, not only brings me into an acceptable relationship with God but also gives me a new nature that is able to please God.

When I sense that I have the constant presence of God within me, all the problems that I once thought were of tremendous importance now fit into an entirely new and different perspective. When spiritual values take their rightful place, and when my relationship with Christ becomes all-important, then "the things of earth grow strangely dim in the light of His glory and grace."

Nearly 800 years before Christ came to earth, speaking through the Prophet Isaiah, God stated mankind's greatest problem and, at the same time, presented the solution: "Come now, and let us reason together, saith the Lord: though your sins be as scarlet (the problem), they shall be as white as snow (the solution)" (Isaiah 1:18). This God does through Christ's death on the cross and through His subsequent resurrection.

Today, the Bible assures us that "if thou shalt confess with thy mouth the Lord Jesus, and shalt believe in thine heart that God hath raised Him from the dead, thou shalt be saved" (Romans 10:9).

Speaking of the Lord Jesus Christ, Apostle John says ". . . His own received him not. But as many as received him, to them gave he power to become the

118

sons of God, even to them that believe on his name: which were born, not of blood, nor of the will of the flesh, nor of the will of man, but of God" (John 1:11-13).

And this leads us to Jesus' statement to Nicodemus on the necessity of being born again: "Marvel not that I said unto thee, ye must be born again" (John 3:7).

There is only one way to find peace with God; there is only one way to be at peace with yourself and your neighbor; there is only one way to get rid of guilt; there is only one way to have power over sin; there is only one way to go to heaven, and that is by being born a second time. A spiritual birth qualifies us for membership in God's family.

If you believe this, then ask Christ to be born in you. As you finish the last chapter of this book, you can begin a new chapter in your own life. And the story of your life will be one of fascination and adventure as you walk with God. For you will have accepted God's solution—Jesus—to your number one problem—sin.